I'm not a Paki

Susan Vickers

I'm not a Paki
ISBN: 978-1-3999-2088-9

First published in Great Britain
in 2022 through Amazon self-publishing
service Kindle Direct Publishing

Disclaimer: The disclaimer is to say only some of the names and places have been changed.

Produced by samanthahoughton.co.uk

Dedication

For my sister Carole.

Thank you for sharing your mom and dad who in turn became mine too. For the struggles and pain, you endured for just being my sister and for being the epitome of the saying, 'family is not always blood.'

I love you.

And for everyone who is struggling with self-loathing - remember it's not you it's them. No one else is you and that's your super power. People fall in love with your soul not your colour.

For anyone who has ever been a bully, a racist or has hatred in their hearts for others - the world is changing, are you?

Contents

Dedication	3
Acknowledgements	6
Foreword	9
Praise For "I'm not a Paki."	11
Author Bio	13
Prologue	14
We will live on love alone	17
The Path Of True Love	20
"You can take your sister home"	25
Do you eat a lot of chocolate?	29
"We don't have wogs here"	42
Imperial Leather	51
Hanging on the telephone	59
Dangerous Liaisons	71
There's something about Mary	84
Model Behaviour	101
Certifed	121
"Which one are you?"	131
Sister act	154
Inconvenience Store	162
Tony	173
Talking Italian	188
Axe to grind	196
Desperately seeking Susan	206
Connect with me	224

Acknowledgements

First and foremost, I would like to thank my mom and dad...Freda and Raymond Vickers, without you welcoming me into your family, my life may have been much, much worse. Despite the world we lived in, you still wrapped your arms around me as a baby and made me your own. Thank you.

My sister, Carole. Thank you for being a sister I didn't know I needed. The questions and grief you have had to put up with because of my skin colour should not have been a worry a young child should endure. You have been my travel partner for many years worldwide and have been my sidekick on various ventures. Even though people refused to believe we were sisters, you never denied me, even in tough times. I love you.

Terry, my big brother, thank you for just accepting me as your sister, especially as I am way funnier than you.

Adrian Morris, thank you for allowing me the circumstances for me to be me and to be able to write this book and never question why or who I am. I will forever be grateful. I love you.

Ian Henery, you are my confidant and the person who has supported me throughout this process and much more. You are a talented poet, playwright, solicitor and author of the written word yourself. I am lucky to not only call you an associate but, more importantly, my friend, your patience, advice and help as I have entered this world has been so warm and appreciated.

My girls and ODC family, Lisa, Hayley, and Virginia, thank you for being my comfort blanket, safety net, and always making things better. Making me laugh even when I didn't know I needed it. You are the best medicine ever, and your understanding of me during this process has been a joy.

Beth, my girl, there's something about our friendship that heals life. We never fail to laugh so much that we just laugh at ourselves laughing. Thank you for accepting me for me, never wanting anything but friendship, never judging and always being there in any situation. Your life is due to change dramatically, and you will be the best mom ever. I cannot wait to watch you continue to bloom in life.

Emma Harrison, my soul sista, you have always been and will continue to be the most beautiful soul I have ever met. You taught me to see the good in every situation. You live via your soul so naturally. If only everyone in the world had even just a tiny bit of Emma-ness in them, the world would be a more comfortable and beautiful place to live. Finn is the luckiest boy in the world to have you as his mom, and the view of the world you show him will make him a joy for anyone he connects with.

Gary Prescott, I owe so much to you for being the only teacher in high school who took notice and listened. I have never forgotten that. You were a shining example of a compassionate, caring teacher and way ahead of your time. Schools today need more Mr Prescott's.

New York City, USA, you showed me my life without prejudice. You will always feel like home.

To all those who have abandoned, denied, bullied, abused or tormented me throughout my life... without you, this book would not have been possible. You gave me the experience to be able to help others. You showed me what love was not. You made me find my soul and live through it. Now I feel victorious.

My mentor, and now my friend, Samantha Houghton, well, you have held my hand throughout the writing of this book. Without you, I would have not even put pen to paper. It would have just been another year, decade and lifetime before even thinking about it. I am in awe of you and what you have achieved and helped others achieve. You are like an angel who has been sent to guide people to share their stories, and you do it so well. This has been an intense time, but you have been like the shot of goodness we all need. You deserve to be held in love every single day of your life. Thank you, and the journey will continue.

Finally...

To the little girl who did not understand the name-calling, nastiness, the hatred, and the heartache, I see you now, the world sees you now... thank you for holding on, thank you for letting me tell your story, you will continue to rest inside my soul where it's warm and full of love for the rest of our life.

Foreword

A sense of belonging, an identity is something that many of us take for granted. As we grow up it helps us make sense of the world and understand our place in it. We are bound to our communities, and this strength and security allows us to engage with other traditions and cultures. In short it supports and enriches our lives. Imagine that this was taken away from you. To live in a cultural vacuum, where there are lots of questions and very few answers, to be subjected to the cruellest effects of social exclusion. This fantastic book explores this and so much more.

All of us struggle with identity. To understand who we are, what we are and how we should behave. Fortunately, most of us navigate this journey successfully with the support of our family and wider community. We never have to seek acceptance, it's a given. For Susan, this was not, and in some ways is still not her story, which is so expertly told. This is a story of extremes, it will move you and make you ask questions, as all great books do. Some of the content in this book is not an easy read, it may not conform to our cosy, liberal view of life. Susan tells the story with honesty, she does not hide from the truth, and in so doing exposes herself to the readership. That is the reason you need to read this book.

You will learn about what it is like to have to work hard every single day to be accepted. The extreme measures that a young girl, and woman, will go to in order to achieve this. You will learn about the toxic nature of racism in this country. The everyday, relentless and normalised kind that can easily drive a person under. You will learn about a young woman's search for her family, to try and understand her place in the world. To not be a secret.

There is anger in these pages. Why wouldn't there be? But there is compassion, integrity, honesty and love. Everything as humans we aspire to be. If you want to understand why we are what we are, read this book now.

Adrian Morris

Praise For "I'm not a Paki."

I first met Susan Vickers in 2021 at the Willenhall Lock Stock Festival. I knew of her before I met her and I was in awe of her reputation. She has a photo of her and Billy Idol on her social media profile which probably tells you all you need to know about Susan Vickers. She is an amazing lady and I was aware that she had been a broadcaster in New York before taking up residency at the Radio Station.

I also knew of her as a former model and community entrepreneur who had compered the Judgestock Festival only 24 hours before Lock Stock in Wednesbury. Susan was running on adrenalin and I was - and still am - in awe of this human dynamo. I had only put my name forward to perform some poetry at Lock Stock (there was an audience of 3,000 people) but was invited by the organisers to compere with Susan the Pop & Soul Stage. I had enormous trepidation. Susan didn`t need any help and she is the Real Deal - a professional performer, compere and broadcaster and I honestly felt that she didn`t need a poetry sidekick. However, she welcomed me and we discovered a natural rapport. To be asked to write this foreword on her behalf and to be shown the chapters of the book as they were written by Susan is a massive compliment. Thank you, Susan.

What has been revealing since Lock Stock is the other side of Susan which she has revealed in the writing of this book. She has shown enormous candour and bravery in opening up her soul and heart to show us who she really is and to encourage us to embrace ourselves with honesty. In leading by example Susan is asking us to share with our loved ones who we really are and our secret identity. In removing our defensive walls we allow our loved ones to love us more completely.

What I first perceived of Susan Vickers was the public face of a professional broadcaster and not the person behind the mask. Listening to her daily broadcasts on the radio has shown me that she very much wants to help people and empower both her listeners on her radio show and the readers of her book. Susan Vickers is a power of positivity and we need that right now in a world that has been savaged by COVID 19, global climate change. Our generation is tackling existential anguish like none other before it. We need a writer like Susan Vickers to lead the way by example. Let`s lay down our masks and weaponry and open our hearts and embrace the world with honesty. Tomorrow is not guaranteed.

Susan tackles numerous topics in this book and each time shows us what it means to be a survivor and vanquish personal demons and setbacks to spread love and compassion for all. Susan`s story makes us look into our own hearts and see ourselves for who we really are and to make peace with our past.

This is a book that needs to be read and then read again. Susan knows her stuff and writes from personal experience. Her mission has always been to leave her legacy and to help those who are going through similar personal crises. If she can just help one person then I know she would believe it would have been all worth it. I totally recommend this.

Ian Henery, solicitor, poet & playwright
www.ianhenerypoet.com

Author Bio

Susan Vickers is a broadcaster, model, entrepreneur and community champion supporting many local festivals, charities and events.

She broadcasts daily on international radio to over 985k people. She uses her platform to talk about and raise issues many of us struggle through daily.

This book has been over 30 years in the making. With the cultural revolution over the past few years, Susan has finally been able to feel the world is a safer place to talk about her struggles with identity.

Susan uses her experiences to help others by speaking out, highlighting social injustices, and supporting various charities and causes.

Prologue

As I am stood on a motorway bridge in Staffordshire, with the skies above me grey and dull, I look down at the plain, white envelope I'm clutching tightly in my hands. I'm feeling anxious, scared, nervous and hopeful in turn. The contents of the envelope holds the key as to how the rest of my life will pan out.

The traffic noise on this busy stretch of the motorway hums violently beneath me. There is an unlimited number of multi-coloured cars, heavy pounding trucks and lorries that carry daily goods - all just going about their business. They are all oblivious of the person standing on the bridge above them and the soul whose heart is breaking.

For 21 years, I had hoped for the 'happy ever after' of a bright, joyful future and everything that I had wished for as a girl growing up who just wanted to be loved and to love in return. Is that so wrong?

The envelope contained the answers I'd been wearily searching for, which helped explain the heartache and destruction that had ravaged not only my life, but also those around me. The best-case scenario would be that the contents of the envelope would put to bed all the heart wrenching pain of the previous 21 years of my life.

I hope so desperately for the words that I long to see that it is felt like a physical pain deep within. I feel the tension and adrenaline chugging through my body; my muscles hurt, my legs are like heavy weights as my heart pounds deep within my soul. I feel hot-cold as the dense heavy energy engulfs me. My head has turned to sensation of cotton wool and iron filings – it cannot be described in any other way. As I stare at the envelope, I find myself trying to telepathically induce good things inside it.

Please don't let it be true! Anything but that… I silently plead to myself. I feel like I'm begging, crying and dying at once.

Maybe if I never opened it I could pretend it's not a thing? I could carry on living my life without the raging curiosity, the all-consuming needing to know and without the hope for everything to be different. Could I do that?

I pleaded and implored to the grey scudding clouds of diesel fumes that swirled around me on that bridge. I want it to just go away and not to be a thing. I don't want my worst fear to be confirmed. I long not to care and everyone else not to care. I don't want any of this!

But the answer, if I really ever expected an answer - was just the roar of the traffic below that bridge as they sped away into the distance, whilst I made deals with the universe.

Maybe I should rip it up without opening it, like they do in the movies and live out my 'happily ever after'? Isn't it safer to know nothing? Isn`t ignorance bliss? What good would ever come from opening the plain white envelope?

Would it provide me with some form of euphonic alignment? Perhaps there would be an internal beam of light that shoots out from within my soul and up to the sky and make everything better? Yeah right.

Is the world just better off without me? My soul could fall from the motorway bridge onto the tarmac below, taking with it my heart, internal organs and my life. What if my whole being pixelates into black dust and disappears into the wind? What if I lost the use of every limb in my body, my speech and the service of my mind?

Even worse - what if the contents of the envelope mean I have to continue to live the rest of my life the way it has been up to now?

CHAPTER ONE

We will live on love alone

Freda was so maternal she felt she was born to care for little ones, especially babies; she loved children but after desperately trying to conceive naturally, the diagnosis of an early menopause shattered that dream. With so much love to give and a huge heart bursting to the brim, she and Raymond decided they would like to foster children, with the hope to provide love to young ones who were less fortunate in this world.

Raymond was born in 1928 and one of two siblings to humble beginnings in Yorkshire, a young 14-year-old man lied to join the British Army. He served the UK with pride for 25 years as a Sergeant in the21st Lancers and a tank driver. This took him all over the world, albeit primarily stationed in Singapore for most of the years, giving him that wonderfully envied tan and mesmerising, blue eyes. This well-versed gentlemen and small-time ladies' man decided it was probably time he settled down, found himself a wife, and became a family man.

Freda Doris Pickett was born in 1938, one of three girls and a brother. She took to farming life in the English countryside like a duck to water. Enjoyed the hilly bike rides, the fresh eggs from the chickens and the freshness of the country air in the beautiful countryside of Claverley, whilst dwelling in a very tiny, tightly packed cottage. The money was tight but the love was deep in such a warm, loving family home.

After many years in service looking after children and helping a local doctor look after their house, it was love at first sight upon walking into a cafe that Freda Doris Pickett first laid eyes on the enigmatic Raymond Frederick Charles Vickers back in 1960. Despite standing just a few inches taller than her new beau Freda was totally in love so much that just six months had passed when she assertively stated the words "don't you think it's about time we got married." And so, it was... With the army paying a pittance and money in service meagre, Freda asked the question,

"We have no money; what will we do?"

Raymond looked into her eyes and lovingly said, "We will live on love alone."

A few months to the end of 1960, and holding a silver horseshoe with a black cat token for luck, adorning her white flowing gown, they walked out of Saint Peters Church in Wolverhampton. Arm in arm with smiles on their faces, and a whole future ahead of them they hasted into a car to honeymoon in Blackpool UK.

Ray left the army, and the newly-weds settled down in a modest house in Wolverhampton. 1961 saw the birth of their first child, a bouncing bundle of joy which they called Carole Ann. Freda was so maternal; she loved children, particularly babies a she was the youngest of four herself, so she was happy so happy to finally be a mother.

The happily married couple wanted many children; however, it was not meant to be. After so many attempts of trying, and many draining spells in hospital, the realisation that they would not be bearing any more children of their own was heart breaking. So, the idea of parenting others bloomed.

And so, the process began. With all procedures and checks complete, it was time to open their arms and doors for their first foster child. It didn't matter size, shape, colour, or personality; they loved them all. Freda and Raymond had ten incredible years of fostering so many babies, toddlers and even teenagers. Every one of them were welcomed into the small but adequate loving home of Freda, Ray and Carole.

The swinging 60s were almost over, leaving many children of mixed-race Jamaican, African, Asian and all different races, from all walks of life in care and social services were finding it so hard to place these children, as no one would look after them in fear of retribution or disdain from society. However, Freda and Ray didn't see skin colour; all they saw were children needing someone to care for them and love; they welcomed all children with open arms without a thought of anyone else's opinion.

CHAPTER TWO

The Path Of True Love

Elsewhere, living as a twenty-something single mother in the early 1970s, Pamela had a bubbly personality, big blonde hair and an infectious smile. Pamela found herself in the throes of young love with dark-haired, olive-skinned Tony. He whisked her off her feet as they enjoyed the euphoric highs of the honeymoon phases of love, with stolen kisses and unrelenting passion.

With Pamela's loving mother taking care of her first child. Pamela and Tony found themselves in the excitement of a brand-new relationship. Tony was the most handsome man Pamela had ever seen, and despite living in a tiny bedsit and not a single penny to their name, their world was their own, and they lived and loved like no one else existed. It was true love. They were young and carefree and didn't care about the disapproving looks that they got; they didn't care that Tony's family didn't want them to be together. The racial and religious differences were so much to bear, but Pamela and Tony didn't care; they loved hard, they loved deeply, and no one else, and nothing else mattered. Life was a bit of a fairy tale.

Upon Tony's return from work, Pamela sat Tony down on the bed.

"I'm pregnant", Pamela said with excitement but trepidation, "what are we going to do?"

"My parents won't like it," said Tony.

"We've got to tell them," said Pamela.

"We can't tell them," said Tony.

So many questions ran through their minds. Tony seemed scared, shocked and unsure how to act; however, Pamela was strong, in love and was a fierce lady.

"I don't care we're in love. Who cares?" she proclaims.

Tony, coming from a huge family where family and relations within were so tight, knew it would never be accepted; they already weren't. So, bringing an interracial child into his family, who was not one of their 'own', would cause them to be shamed. This would extend from the family, to friends and everyone who ever existed.

"We will never be accepted," he said, "but you know what, I'm young, I'm free, and I love you, let's get married," Tony said.

Pamela's eyes grew more expansive than they had ever been before, almost like the craters we see on the moon that, despite being so many miles away, can still be seen from earth. Her heart was ready to explode with sheer love, elation and joy like she had never felt before. She flung her arms around him; the smile on his face dazzled her, and his arms around her waist as he spun her around, assuming the answer was yes. They pulled apart but still smiling Pamela said, "but we can't, how are we going to do this? No one will let it happen".

"We'll find a way", said Tony. "I don't care; let's just do it. We love each other, don't we? And that's all that matters."

As the bells chimed and the confetti fell, the church steps were graced with glee and joy. Pam was in a beautiful white dress and Tony in a grey suit slightly too big for him. Still, nonetheless, the smile on his face distracted from the fact that only a handful of people attended the ceremony. No one wanted to be seen accepting the marriage of two people who shouldn't be together in the eyes of their families and societies, let alone two people from differing faiths. Still, they didn't care; they had married, and everyone else's thoughts, prejudices and religious beliefs didn't matter today in their heads; this was the happiest day of their lives.

Sharing a tiny bedsit with a few other people was such a tight squeeze for Tony and a pregnant Pamela. People were coming and going at all hours, and it was not the right environment for a young family to start life. The weeks and the months soon passed until their daughter was born. Pamela and Tony became parents of a beautiful, bouncing baby girl with big brown eyes and lots of brown hair, just like her dad. Their new life was about to begin.

"How are we going to cope," said Pamela

"We'll find a way", replied Tony.

Pamela's family were overjoyed with another baby being bought into the family. However, Tony's family still had their eyebrows raised disapprovingly. Pamela would do anything for the love that she had for Tony. She would do anything to have Susan accepted by all the family, especially his family. However, money was tight, times were tough, and arguments were starting to become part of the daily routine; raising a newborn baby in a tiny bedsit with a few other people was hard. Plus, the early 70s was a tough financial time for the country.

"We can't buy nappies, we can't buy baby food, and Susan is now 3 months old; how are we going to cope?" Pamela asked.

"I don't know, we need to get ourselves right before anything else, we need to find ourselves a stable home, good jobs and have money

coming in for ourselves before we can look after a child."
Pamela's heart was torn. She'd already got a child being looked after by her own mother; she could not ask her to look after Susan too, but with no way of finding a job to bring an income in during tough times, what could they do? Finally, Tony sat Pamela down and said,

"We must give Susan up; we can't cope."

"No, there's no way I can do that," said Pamela, heartbroken.
"But you love me, don't you, Pamela?" said Tony
He continued with gusto, "We will put Susan into care whilst we sort ourselves out."

Pamela was shocked; how could he suggest such a thing? Tony explained, "We will never be able to just put her in to care for a couple of months; we will need longer than that. So maybe the best thing that we can do is put Susan up for adoption because the process of adoption takes years to go through. During that time, we will be free to find ourselves somewhere nice to live, to have some money coming in and get ourselves back on track and then we can get her back before the process of actually being adopted starts".

"No, no," said Pamela ", we can't do that. She is our daughter; we are a family."

Weeks went by, no decision was made, but the arguments had increased, and the times got more challenging. Susan was a baby just a few months old who was crying, teething, and needing nappies and food, both of which were unaffordable. Still, Pamela loved Tony so much so, so much she would do anything, just anything for him, anything to be a happy family.

"Could I really give up my child? Just for a short time, of course, maybe?" Pamela thought to herself, "I do love him so much, and it would make him happy; it could work" Pamela was so confused, indecisive and struggled to make sense of her inner turmoil.

Arguments got louder and more frequent, but they both continued to try and make things work. However, with seemingly no light at the end of the tunnel, one afternoon Tony said, "I'm just taking Susan to go and see my family".

He had to do this by himself as Pamela wasn't welcome. Tony was trying his best to make amends and make things right with his family. Pamela saw it as progress and she needed the break, so she told him she loved him and off he went.

Tony returned later that day empty-handed.

"Have you left Susan with your family?" questioned Pamela confused. "No said Tony, I haven't.

CHAPTER THREE

"You can take your sister home"

In 1970 a 3-month-old baby girl was bought to the home of Freda and Ray to be cared for after being left at social services; as always, Freda's raised arms were open and welcoming, this baby was to be a resident in the family home, as a lot of children were just daycares or weekends, but this little girl had the biggest bedroom of her own, and it was the biggest bedroom in the whole house.

Weeks went by, months went by, and the care and the love continued. It was always hard giving back the children that they cared for as many were placed in their care for many different reasons. Some were born from addicts, some were placed in their care because they were abandoned, sometimes their parents were sent to prison. There were many reasons some of these parents' made recoveries or were in better situations, but they were able to come and get their children back.

However, in this particular baby girls' case, no one came back for her. It was sad that this baby girl who, through no fault of her own, was abandoned. There was no news, no curiosity or interest by the birth parents, there was nothing. So, Freda and Ray just continued on relentlessly being the best foster parents to this abandoned baby girl. Until one day, the social worker came to visit.

"Not sure how long Susan will be staying with you now as she's going up for adoption", the social worker stated with a heavy heart, as she knew how fond they were of Susan.

They had loved this baby girl, a whole year with teething, screaming,

crying, laughing, loving and doing everything together as if she was their own. Even the then 9-year-old sister was enjoying having a baby sister, which she never thought she'd have. Susan was cared for by these foster parents as though she was born to them, as though they were her real mom and dad, which then made them ask a very important question and a question that would change everybody's life forever.
"Can we adopt her?"

After many unsuccessful attempts to have another natural child, this was like a blessing in disguise. They already loved her; she already felt like their own. Recalling the emotion and heartbreaks of handing back so many children to their natural parents, which they'd cared for over the years, indeed, this was the answer to all of their prayers. They wanted her to be their daughter; they wanted to be her actual mom and dad.

After having fostered for almost 10 years the process of adopting was swift and just a few months later they found themselves standing in a cold walled high ceiling stone court room, with so many officials in suits and capes milling around them and hardly anyone speaking to them, they knew they were being judged. Freda, Raymond and Carole stood in silence besides an oblivious bundle of blankets wrapped around a baby who unusually was very quiet ... she had a biscuit in her hands which always kept her content.

"You can take your sister home," said the judge to Carole with a vast, satisfactorily smile on his face.

Now 18 months old, Susan was no longer the abandoned baby needing love; she was no longer in the system to be passed around for 16 years like the unwanted gift no one has a place for. She now had a mum and dad who wanted and loved her. Notices we put in the local newspapers telling the world this baby girl was no longer a foster child. She was officially their daughter, albeit an adopted daughter but a daughter nonetheless.

Whilst receiving this news brought much joy within the family home Freda and Ray were not expecting things would change around them. Other family members were always totally fine and pleased with Freda and Ray fostering children; they were doing a good thing, looking after these children that no one wanted as it didn't really affect them and their 'standing' in society in the slightest. But now, this baby girl who had brown skin was an official and legal member of their family; she was their niece, cousin, and distant relative. Not just family members, outside of the house this brown-skinned baby was someone's neighbour, someone's, friend's daughter, someone that lived in their street, someone's child who went into their shop.

The 70's were the days that people loved to stop a mother in the streets upon seeing them pushing one of those huge carriage prams, to peer inside, only to then have their face retorted in disgust and shock when realising it was not a bouncy giggly white/pinkish child as expected. The questioning looks, frowns and raised eyebrows of people looking at the white-skinned mum, the white skinned dad, the white-skinned first-born with a brown-skinned baby. Their disapproving reactions were not always verbal, before trotting away at speed in case they caught the plague.

Some family members stopped coming to the house, and the usual chats with window cleaners or milkmen stopped. It was with much dismay and frustration to Freda and Ray that a certain close family member finally spoke up to express their feelings stating, "You will have nothing but trouble having one of those."

Where did all this come from? She was just a baby. Everyone was perfectly fine with them looking after mixed-race children when they knew they would be handed back. Now, this brown-skinned baby was a part of the family meaning their family too; it was like they had bought the devil himself into their lives. Freda and Ray had to let it wash over them as much as possible; the '70s were rife with 'The National Front', as it had not been that long since racism was made an offence, but so many people would not accept it. Freda and Ray didn't care what anybody thought, this baby girl was loved, she was going to continue to be loved, and she was now their daughter.

CHAPTER FOUR

Do you eat a lot of chocolate?

The Mid 70s, was when I attended the local primary school on my council estate. With my mom tightly grasping my hand, we'd walk past the precinct of shops and through a large park which consisted of two smaller parks known locally as 'top park' and 'bottom park'. It was about a 20-minute walk.

I do not remember too much from the very early years, but when I look back at photographs now, I must have stood out like a sore thumb. I can only recall 2 other children of colour, both of which were Jamaican, in the whole school; there was no one else that I remember that looked like me.

We didn't have much money. My mum and dad gave up fostering after adopting me, as between myself and my sister having a bedroom, there was no room to take on more children. My dad was a full-time roof lagger, and my mom used to clean people's houses whilst I was at school. We had help from the government to pay for our school uniforms, so the clothing that myself and my sister wore was all we could afford with hand me downs, and second-hand clothes that we would 'grow into', which always meant they would never fit.

I didn't have any friends at primary school; no one wanted to play with me, no one wanted to be seen with the person everyone looked at strangely, that everyone just gawped at. There were always groups of parents walking to school together, laughing and joking, but it was always just mum and me on our own, and that was OK. Until I was adamant, I was grown up enough to walk to school independently, feeling like a big girl. "I can walk on my own", I said to my mum, thinking this might be why people looked at me and whispered or sniggered, "oh, your mom still brings you to school", I'd hear them say amongst other things.

So gradually, my mom started stopping at the bottom of the park and watching me walk up the park safely on my own. Then a week later, she'd stop by the shops and watch me walk a little bit further safely, and then she'd walk just to the end of the street by our house to make sure I got off OK. However, I still had no friends, no one wanted to walk with me, so I made that journey on my own with my satchel. "Do you eat a lot of chocolate?" one girl said to me.

"No, why?" I replied.

"Well, my mum said that you eat a lot of chocolate, and that's why you're that colour."

As I said before, money was very tight in our house. Still, my mum always made sure there was a meal on the table at teatime, whether a bowl of soup with some bread and butter or crispy pancakes which were my favourite. Hence, bars of chocolate were a total luxury which were very, very few and far between, except the selection box at Christmas, which was always a treasure. Upon getting home from school, I questioned my mum "Sally asked me if I ate a lot of chocolate, is that why I'm this colour because I've had a bar of chocolate?"

My mom giggled and replied, "No, just ignore her."

And that was it - that was the end of the conversation; no other explanation or clarification was made; she just found it funny.

I thought nothing of it until another time in school, a group of kids came up to me laughing and teasing me, "Don't you have a wash?"

"Yes", I snapped back, "but you have got dirt all over you."

Knowing I hadn't been by the sandpit or down the bank in the playground, the only dirt mark I could see was where the boot Polish from my shoes had rubbed off on my ankle socks as we sat cross-legged in assembly each day. So, I'd lick my thumb and forefinger and try rubbing at my skin. No, it definitely was not dirt; I knew it was not dirt even though we were only allowed a bath on a Sunday ready for school the next day. I still had to have a 'strip wash' every day before and after school. I scrubbed my skin with one of those wooden hard-bristled nail brushes and pumice stones that were used to get hard skin off people's feet until I was raw red. Upon noticing these marks, my mother asked, "what's all this on your skin"?

To which I told her I'm trying to get this colour off; it just won't come off; it's dirt."

"No, it's not dirt; that's the colour of your skin", replied my mum.

Home life was very, very strict in our house, my parents were old school. In their generation, children were would only speak when spoken to, we had to sit and be quiet. We weren't allowed to play noisy games. However, I had very few games, as for most you needed more than one person to play, and I didn't have friends; my sister was nine years older than me, and she didn't want to play with a kid; she had her own interests. This was an age where there wasn't the technology we have today; you had to literally entertain yourself. So, I was fabulous at colouring and even entered many colouring competitions in the local newspaper. I won quite a few times. A singing Smurf was my favourite winning prize. The funny thing is there were two winners of this singing Smurf in a colouring competition in the local paper, and it wasn't until I was in my early 20s that, by chance, I ended up dating the brother of the other girl that won the other Smurf, oh we did laugh. Another time I won tickets to see The Jungle Book at the cinema, oh so excited. Still, I had no friends to go with, "find a friend", said my father.

"No one will be my friend", I replied.

It wasn't that easy to just go out and get a friend, so I ended up going with the girl next door, they were a religious family who were white of course. There were free tickets to see the latest film in town it was an exciting thing, so we went along and enjoyed the movie.

During my primary school years, I had a growth spurt. I shot to probably one of the tallest in my year, albeit short-lived. I was one of the first to wear a bra; this was to much amusement for the other kids because they could see the outline of my bra through my thin school shirt and cardigan, so everybody started to twang the strap. I remember the teacher called Mr Jarocki, who used to shout in the playground for kids to stop picking on me, which I found terrific, but he never stopped them from picking on me for everything else. So now things were distracted a little from the colour of my skin, the names we're still going on, "are you a Paki"

"No" I'd reply harshly, not even knowing what that meant.

Still, the chants and the names continued, in the playground, after school, walking to school, and now I was being picked on for wearing a bra. There were some girls who dragged me into the toilets and lifting my shirt up to see what it looked like and then continuing to lift my bra off to see if there was a reason, I was actually wearing one!

Strangely it just felt like a change or almost a light relief to being bullied and picked on for something other than the colour of my skin. Because we grow up surrounded by adults, we already have an idea what's to come. We know we're going to grow taller, we know we're going to grow boobs, we know we're going to wear high heels and makeup, so we know what's to come as it's expected. So, I could deal with that to a point, but looking so different to everyone else was something incomprehensible, and I didn't understand it. I didn't know how to deal with it, but I knew it was ugly. I knew it was a horrible thing, and it was a bad thing. I knew it made people angry.

Because home life was so strict, there were never many conversations within the household. Whenever my mum and dad argued, my sister and I would be sent upstairs to our bedrooms out of the way, so we weren't party to it; however, we still heard everything. One of the only times that I had my mum to myself was if we went over to the shops together. Still, then my mum being the friendly person she was, would spend a few minutes in every shop chatting to the people that worked there, that is the way things were back then, people seemed a lot more friendly to everyone.

I can remember the first early conversations with my mom in 1977, specifically 16th August. We had a coal fire back then, and we hated it, we hated the mess it caused every morning. Ironically people now love a coal fire or a log burner in the house. I used to sit in front of the fire first thing in the morning. We had no central heating, so the coal fire would heat the boiler at the back of the fire. Hence, we had hot water. We also had a really noisy electric heater that got wheeled into each bedroom just before bedtime to heat the room and 'take the edge off'. So, one of the only times mom and I would be just the two of us, would be when I would get up in the morning and sit in front of the coal fire to warm up.

This one particular morning, I remember watching the telly (which was Rediffusion and had to be turned over by a switch on the window sill, which is unimaginable today), everyone was constantly talking about this man who had died; everybody was crying, they were so sad. My mother was transfixed by the TV, it was on the news, it was on all the programs, all the channels, this man called Elvis is dead, with the headlines Elvis, Elvis, Elvis on almost everything that we watched. It was a colossal talking point everywhere. I watched these scenes on the TV in confusion. I remember clearly asking my mother who it was, and mum trying to explain to me he was a tremendous singer, he was a very well-loved man and he had a great voice. I couldn't understand why the whole world were losing their minds over this one person that I'd never heard of. Of course, now I get it, but as a 7-year-old child, I couldn't understand it.

That was the first mother with a daughter conversation that I remember. The only other time I remember having a conversation with her was when I was sitting in exactly the same place. She was also sitting in precisely the same position on 'dad's chair'. We were only allowed to sit on dad's chair when he was in bed or out. Only this time, the question I asked wasn't about anything on the telly; it was about me.

"Why does everybody call me names? Why doesn't anyone like me? Why I am so different?"

"Because your parents were different" was the reply from Mom; this made me more confused, as my parents seemed like everyone else's to a point. "But I don't see anyone calling them names or saying anything to them." And that's when my mom said, "but we aren't your real parents"

"Yes, you are", I replied.

"No, we adopted you, but your real parents were dark, foreign" Mom Said

"Oh, so you're not my real mom and dad,"?

"No", Mom replied, "and people don't understand that", she continued.

As a 7-year-old child, I didn't understand that explanation, but I knew not to keep asking questions as everything just felt... kind of awkward. "And you should just ignore anyone who says anything." she added.

And that was that. I thought nothing much of it, mainly because I didn't know what she was talking about, and I also didn't understand that that explanation would not stop the name-calling and the bullying at school.

I saw two people, a boy and a girl, in the top year classes at primary school in the playground, they were with loads of friends around them, laughing and joking and playing together, and they were darker than me. Although not knowing their parent's heritage at the time, they were Jamaican, but they were so much darker than me it made no sense. My skin was slightly lighter, yet I was called names in the playground. No one would play with me. No one would even sit next to me in the class. Why was I so hated?

The classrooms consisted of single and double tables where two people could sit together. People would scurry to the desks whenever class was called, to sit next to their friends or by the window. Or anywhere else but by the brown-skinned girl. I'd see people telling people to sit next to him because they didn't want me sitting there. If there was the only vacant spot in some classes for me to sit, I would be next to someone I would see then move their chair as much away from me as possible or complain to the teacher. It was like either my colour would rub off onto them, or they didn't want to catch the brown.

As the months and years went by in primary school, I noticed cliques, groups, and gangs were starting to form. Kids would start to develop in certain areas in the playground. So, I would always make sure I didn't walk by them because if I did, I'd have a whole load of abuse and name-calling, sometimes things thrown at me. Laughing with each person trying to say something more funny or provocative than the previous one.

I knew people didn't like me because of my skin colour. I didn't understand it, but I knew that was the reason. So how can I make people like me? I'd watch people and I would watch all the other kids, the way they dressed, the way they did their hair, but I couldn't copy them. I had no choice in how I dressed as my uniform was bought with tokens from the government, and the option was minimal. So, my hair always looked greasy because we couldn't really afford a shampoo. Still, every now and then, we would have one sachet of Lincoln beer shampoo from the chemist, which was very cheap and that one sachet would have to do the whole family. Failing that, it was washing up liquid. As a result, my hair was always greasy and mostly pulled into two pigtails on either side of my head, until I reached about 9-10 years old. I was pretty tall for my age, we couldn't afford a hairdresser, so mom used to cut our hair; I had a fringe halfway up my forehead, all wonky like she'd cut it with a spoon, and really short into my neck at the back of my head, so it was easier to manage. So now, not only did I look different to everyone else because of my skin colour and now because looked like a boy as well.

But there had to be another way to make people like me. I had free school meals, we couldn't afford pocket money, so I wasn't allowed treats or packed lunches, so our school meals were free, but I noticed lunchtime was when everybody got together and had a laugh and sat down together eating. Well, everyone else did. They were sharing plates of food, crisps and sweets out of their lunch boxes. And I noted it was a real bonding friendship kind of thing, but I had nothing to give and nothing to share.

Then I had an idea.

There was always some small change sitting on the mantle-piece at home, where my dad emptied his pockets after work, or my mum had put the milk money on the side. One morning before school, I took (stole) just a few coins off the top; it couldn't have been any more than 50 pence, possibly even less, but it was enough for me to go to the tuck shop at school during break time and buy as many crisps and sweets as I could, which back in the 70s was a fair few packets. With my arms so full I could barely hold everything, I said to one girl who I didn't even know, "would you like a packet of crisps"?

"Yes", not even a please, but I didn't care, her face lit up!

I gave her a choice of any. A friend of the girl said to her, "where did you get those?"

"Susan gave them to me", she replied.

I instantly saw another potential friendly face, "would you like a packet too?"

"Yes, please"

And just like that, the warmth that I felt just for those few seconds was like liquid gold to me. I threw the girl a packet of snaps. However, she took them and ran to tell a few other people, "Susan's got loads of sweets and crisps".

Within seconds I was surrounded by what seemed so many people in the playground. More people than ever wanted to be around me, but this time in a positive way. I knew they didn't want to speak to me or really be my friend but wanting a packet of sweets or packet of crisps for free, but nonetheless, they were happy to be seen with me, they were happy just for those few seconds and to have something from me as a one-off. But for those few moments, I had the golden ticket everyone wanted. I'd cracked the jackpot; no matter what, I looked like I had something they wanted and to get it, they had to be nice to me or just like me, even just for that one second.

Of course, it was all over and done within a matter of minutes, and the school bell rang, and we were back in class, and it was standard service resumed. That felt so good it felt so good, but it was so short-lived.

The teachers contacted my parents knowing that what happened in the playground and the mere fact that I was spending so much money (a small amount of cash) was very unusual.

"We would just like to let you know that Susan had some money today in school and she bought a lot of sweets and chocolate"

My parents hit the roof, putting two and two together after realising the milk money was short.

"I don't know why I did it"

To which they replied." if you want chocolate, just ask for it," which of course, I know that if ever I did that, it would be a definite no.

I had to get knocked down by a car before I was allowed chocolate off the Christmas tree...but that's another story. But I couldn't explain to them the real reason why I did it. So, I just said I don't know why I did.

As the weeks and months went by, of course, everything remained the same, name-calling, bullying, pushing in the corridors, and pulling up my hair. But I was still watching people, who were liked and popular, and most time, the people in classes who were the most disruptive and the troublemakers had the most friends. So even though they were naughty, answering the teacher back, not doing the homework, throwing things across the classrooms, etc., it was all terrible behaviour, still, their friends and the rest of the class would laugh and find it so funny. People laughed at me too, but not because they liked me, but because they felt big calling me names, and it would make their own friends laugh. But, of course, I couldn't steal money from my parents again, so what can I do to make people notice me or like me?

It was this time of year that we sometimes had really terrible blizzards. They were so bad that we couldn't walk through the park to get to school, or the heating wouldn't work sufficiently enough in school, and we would be sent home early, or it wouldn't be open at all. Everybody loved that; everybody was happy when they thought the school wasn't going to be opening, or if they didn't have to go to school, everyone wished for the snow to fall so they could get sent home. That's it! I thought that's what I'd do. I will do something that will make me be noticed for making the whole school like me. But, of course, I couldn't make snow or create blizzards, so how am I going to get the school shut down so we can all be sent home and they can all love me.

As I raised my hand in the air during class, "Sir can I go to the toilet please"

"Yes", said the teacher.

I went to the toilet, washed my hands and then everything rushed into my head, that's it! So that's what I'll do! As I dried my hands with the rough green paper towels in the girl's toilets. I'll just let them drop in the sink under the running water, not one but two and three, turn both taps on. If the school had a flood, we would to be sent home; everyone would be happy, and I would have been the one who made them happy. And that's what I did, I just walked out of the toilet, leaving the taps running and the plugs blocked with the green paper towels. I just returned to class and sat back at my desk calmly, knowing I was about to make everyone like me.

Before the end of the lesson, a teacher came round the classrooms asking if anyone has anyone been to the toilet in the last half an hour, to which everyone pointed and looked at me "Susan."

I was hauled by my arm from the classroom to see the headmistress, the scariest of all teachers. Mrs Cattermole was a little old lady, so she appeared, but we all thought she was a witch; she had a giant cane as these were the days that you could be caned with your tights down too. I was screaming and pulling on every classroom door to stop the teacher from pulling me to the headmistress, shouting, "please don't tell my mum, please, don't tell my mum I didn't do anything."

Someone had obviously gone to the toilet not long after me and scuppered my plans. How had this gone so terribly wrong??

"Why did you do that?" asked the teachers.

"I don't know," I said.

I couldn't explain to anyone the real reason why, I couldn't explain that I wanted people to like me. It made no sense to anyone else saying it out loud. They would never understand; even I didn't really understand, my mom was called into the school. I had to sit on the naughty mat, a brown prickly rough mat by the school's front doors where everybody wipes their feet, and my punishment was to sit on the naughty mat every break time and lunchtime until the end of term. So now I wasn't only feeling isolated in the playgrounds and in classes; I was now physically isolated and on the naughty mat until the end of primary school.

CHAPTER FIVE

"We don't have wogs here"

After leaving the uncomfortableness of primary school, it was now time to go to big school, it's going to be a fresh start, fresh people and new beginnings. Time to leave behind all the trauma, abuse and bullying, name-calling and everything in my primary school. The high school will be good; it's going to be great; no one will notice all the things that the little kids noticed.

However, with my uniform still coming from the government, the material was itchy and cheap and not well-fitting. The shoes were T bars and not very comfortable, despite weeks of walking around the house to 'break them in', and then, of course, I had the duffle coat, the horrendous duffle coat, that my arms were nowhere to be seen, and big enough for me to smuggle the whole street inside. But as mother said, "you will grow into it. It's got to last money doesn't grow on trees."

So, after the obligatory first day of school photograph outside our mid terraced council house, it was off to school I went. Despite all of us first years having a school tour in the previous weeks, the school still felt like the most enormous building in the world. It was very stark, bland and cold; there were stairs everywhere, three floors, three buildings, and none of the doors to the classrooms had titles of classes on, there were no signs at all, yet we were all just thrown into crowds of older boys and girls.

"Just ask any of the other children for directions; if you're lost, they'll be happy to help," said one of the teachers.

We felt like small fish in a vast pond, so insignificant and definitely not noteworthy. I found my class, 'Form 13', typical; of course, it was. This would be the same class with the same people for the rest of my school days. As in primary school, as soon as the teacher unlocked the door to the classroom, everyone shot in super-fast to find the best desk or to sit with their friends, and just like primary school, all the desks were singular or double desks, where just you and one other person could sit. I had no friends, even people I knew from primary school who were in the same class weren't my friends, so I had no need to rush into class like everyone else to make sure I sat next to a friend.

Needless to say, that I was pushed to be the very last person entering this room anyway. As I looked around the room nervously, searching desperately for an empty chair, ideally on my own, there were none to be seen; everyone seemed to be looking at me, some with relief that there were no spaces by them, and some with satisfaction that they just found a vacant space.

"Come on, find somewhere to sit," said the teacher as I was the only person left standing.

"There's nowhere to sit", I replied; I heard some of the kid's sniggers. "Well, find somewhere", said the teacher as I stood the front of the class still by the entrance door.

I was just frozen to the spot as I looked at all the white faces just staring at me, just hoping that they wouldn't be moved by the teacher so I could sit there. Then I heard a scraping of a chair on the hard wooden floors.

"You can sit here," said the girl.

It was like I had been sent an Angel from the gods, and a vacant space came out of seemingly nowhere. I rushed to sit next to my saviour. High school had begun.

The first weeks were spent nervously scurrying between classes around the school finding our feet, memorising the layout. I was hoping that every class had my saviour in so I felt like I had someone who was OK with me sitting next to them, but this was not the case.

"You will make friends," said my mum trying to reassure me when I told her no one wanted to sit with me.

She didn't know how I felt, and I couldn't explain to her; she was always my mum; as kids, we always seemed to forget that our elders went to school and had a lot of similar experiences.

As the weeks and months passed by, not much had really changed from primary school apart from playtimes were now called break times, and everyone seemed to be like skyscrapers around us. Many of the same children from my primary school were now there too. So, the abuse, name-calling and teasing continued; only now it would filter through to so many more people. All the teachers and staff were white, and all the children that I could see too were white, apart from the few in the higher years, the same few from my primary school, and they still had many friends which they laughed and joked within the corridors and dining rooms.

I was actually quite clever at school and in many of the top classes for each subject. English, biology, geography, and history were my favourite subjects, oh the irony. It seemed the only things I had in common with some other children in my classes were the uniforms. Styles were very similar to mine, which meant they were subsidised by the government, meaning others would be picked on for that, the same as me, which gave me a little bit, all be it a very tiny bit, of relief.

P.E. lessons - no one enjoyed them. So, when someone was chosen to pick out their team, I was always the last one standing, so it was with groans and sighs that I had to join specific groups out of no other choice. But then I became very good at sports, netball, rounders and hockey; I did really well, so then as the years went by, I was no longer the last to be chosen as I was now being selected on my skills to catch a ball or to run faster than everyone else and that felt good. Until the changing rooms communal showers, I understand this was a traumatic time for many kids for many reasons. Jointly, many of us didn't like the changing rooms mainly because the P.E. teacher took our towels away from us, forcing us to run naked behind the wall into the communal showers. But a lot of people looked at me for many other curiosities. Usually, people look at each other in the changing room because they want to see if they've started growing hairs on their legs or if they have the big terry-towelling pants on that reach up to our necks. Still, it seemed many people would just stare at me, which at first, I put down to the fact that, like in primary school, I was wearing a bra, and after that experience, that's what I thought at the time. But really, it was one thing seeing a brown face and brown hands, but seeing a brown body too was another thing, and it was amusing for them.

"Does that wash off in the shower?" they would say, and they would watch me to see if I actually used soap and if it would run away down the drain.

In the end, I just got changed as quickly as possible or pretended I needed the toilet and go and get changed in there, but that just made more people more curious, like I had something I definitely had to hide.

As the first year of high school progressed, I started making a few friends. Notably, these were girls that were OK with me sitting next to them in the classroom and sometimes chatting usually about the lesson. However, they were different during break times; they didn't want other people to see them talking to me or being my friend.

Home life was spent with me sitting with my parents' watching television. The Royal Variety shows, Bullseye, or sit in absolute silence as the football scores come in, so my dad could mark the coupons. Sometimes, oddly, my dad would buy me an Airfix model of fighter jets from the war, but I immensely enjoyed sitting at the dining room table doing these.

"Why don't you go out and find some friends?" my dad would say like I could just luckily pick one up off the street or off the shelf in the local shops.

"It's not that easy, dad", I would reply.

The biggest film in history was brought to our screens at the movies in 1982. It was being advertised all over the television, everyone wanted to see it. E.T. The Extra-Terrestrial. Oh my God, I had to see this. I had to see this film, everyone was talking about it at school, it was advertised all the time on the T.V. Then one Saturday, my dad, for the first time ever, gave me some money.

"Go and watch that film." Dad said.

"Who with?" I said

"Take a friend", dad replied

"I have no friends, dad."

"Well, use that money and find one to go with, it will pay for both of you, and I will drop you off and pick you back up again."

Remembering my experience in primary school where I bought everyone sweets to be my friend - yes, this could work. Judy let me sit next to her in biology, so she was my friend; I went to her house and knocked on the door. Judy came to the door.

"My dad has given me some money to go to the pictures. Do you want to come?"

"No, I can't," said Judy, looking confused about why I knocked on her door.

I walked away.

Tracy Griffiths, she's, my friend. We sit together in a couple of classes, and sometimes she lets me sit next to her in the dining room. I walked up the massive drive at the top of our estate. I could see Tracey by the bedroom window at the front of the house. I knocked on the door, her mom answered, pulling the door open quite aggressively.

"Can Tracy come out please?"

"No", snapped her mum.

"I've got some money to go and see E.T. at the pictures; I'm paying," I said.

"She's not in", she snapped and slammed the door in my face.

As I turned to walk what felt like the path of shame for knocking on the door, I could hear muffles from within the house, and then I listened to what must have been the high pitch of her mom's voice, "WE DONT HAVE WOGS HERE."

What did that mean? I had heard that name on T.V. a couple of times, but I didn't really connect it. I went to a few other girl's houses, but with no joy, I went home alone with the money still in my glove.

"What you doing back so soon?" questioned my dad.

"I can't find any friends," I said; I was distraught and disappointed that this time having money didn't work like it did in primary school. "Don't be stupid," said my dad, "when I was your age, I had lots of friends."

This didn't help at all. I couldn't tell him what I heard Tracy's mother say just in case they didn't let me play with her again. Despite what her mother said, I still wanted her as a friend; I didn't have any, so even ones that weren't allowed to be my friend were better than none. These were the years we used to cover our schoolbooks with posters or wallpaper. I didn't have pocket money as a child, but most Fridays, my dad would buy me a magazine to sit at the table in the living room and read to keep me quiet for when the coupon man came around later that night to collect the pools, and he would have a cup of tea with my dad. My mum would be out at bingo. One of my favourite magazines was Look-In, and these always had posters of pop stars on the centre pages. One of my favourite pop groups was Adam and the Ants. I found him just mesmerising because he was so different, and he looked so different, oh the irony. I had his posters up in my bedroom alongside the newly discovered Billy Idol. He was the most beautiful man I had ever seen on TV. My bedroom walls were covered with those posters and my schoolbooks too, that's when I found another novel way of trying to make friends. Some girls in some classes didn't have their books covered, and some had other pop stars on their books, including Adam Ant.

"I haven't got that poster", they would say to me.

"Well, I have two, so I will swap you one for one of yours," I would say in a bid to form some kind of something in common.
"OK", they would say.

It worked again, the old 'I have something you want trick' so I would hastily bring in as many posters as I could off my walls, even the ones I really liked I would sacrifice to obtain a friend, to give to them knowing that they would be thrilled and we would now become the best of friends forever. Only find that they would take all my posters and not give me anything as swaps, not even exchange a conversation. Nicola White did this to me once. So, when I asked for my posters back, she would just call me names until a crowd of her other friends came around her to intimidate me and tell me she would see me at the school gates. Of course, this meant I would be beaten up, so I used to have to hide within a crowd of other kids or walk by a teacher out of the school gates so she wouldn't see me, this kind of thing happened on several occasions.

The first few years of high school were just a continuation of the last few years of primary school; my bag was snatched off me and thrown onto roofs, across playgrounds, people wanting to fight me, so they look significant to others, no one wanted to be my friend or even be seen to be my friend. The only time people actually wanted to sit next to me was during tests because I was always in the top three of the class, so they could try and copy me.

Outside our house was a small wall with the street name on it. Coming home from school one day, I saw my mom with a bucket of suds vigorously washing this wall. I thought this was odd as it was more the neighbour's part of the wall than ours. 'Paki' I could see scrawled in blue paint. I stood staring.

"Never mind what I'm doing, just go in and get washed," my mum said; I knew not to ask any more questions by the tone of her voice, and I think she thought I didn't see it, but I did.

I started noticing quite a few things. I started recognising language, names and anger in society. I also started noticing graffiti across shops shutters, on walls, the same graffiti that I'd see on the news, where people were fighting in the streets, all over the country, people were rioting, setting fire to things. It was in the newspapers my dad would leave around. But what did it mean??

It was just two letters. Who knew 2 letters of the alphabet could cause so much hatred and destruction, pain and trauma.
N.F. National front.

CHAPTER SIX

Imperial Leather

During my early teens, I was able to go over the shops on my own for my mum. But unfortunately, this also meant I had to experience abuse from strangers on my own. Every evening apart from Sundays at 5:15, the local newspaper was delivered to the newsagents, and I was the one that had to go and collect it each night. Why should we pay that extra 50 pence to have delivery when Susan can go and collect it for free, was the thought my mom had. So, whilst she was making tea ready for when my dad returned from work, off I had to go.

I was OK with going and doing errands for my mum, which included going to the shops; what I wasn't OK with was the experiences in doing so. There was a precinct of shops, chemists, grocery stores, hardware, Deli's, chip shop, butchers, newsagents, and a library not far from our house. Outside the library were a row of benches, beautiful mosaic benches left there after a paddling pool was abandoned by the council. Most towns and cities have a gang, meaning a group of young boys and girls who thought they ruled the city, not just the estate; primarily to my knowledge, they would meet up with other gangs and just fight each other or cause general mayhem in and around the area which they lived. There were always whispers and rumours about our local crew, called the Blitz and Subway Army; the talk was always about people being injured and seriously hurt and trouble that they caused not just in our own city but beyond.

I was still too young to know too much about this gang as they mainly consisted of kids around 18/19 years old; however, I did see that they always sat on these benches with people from my school. The benches were situated right outside the newsagents, where I had to purchase the evening paper daily. There wasn't that much to do during these times in the early 80s, unlike today where everyone owns a phone or some kind of technology and computers, and lots of things that mean we generally don't see as many gangs of people hanging around the streets like they used to be. But there wasn't much else to do during these eras except try and cause mayhem around the estates and precincts. So, of course, me going to the shop each day would give way for them to have a few minutes of amusement and a chance for them to show off how tough they were. This consisted of making fun of me for wearing a coat that was way too big for me, my awful haircut or having to wear Wellington boots just because it was raining.

"Oi Paki", they would shout,

"Yeah Paki, you lost?" another would call.

"They don't sell Curry in there" would be another cry.

And then it used to become a competition between themselves to just see who could say something more abusive or funnier than the other. A torrent of abuse would be thrown at me, but being 12 to 13 years old, I had no defence, could not stand up for myself, and could not shout anything back against the big kids. I had to just walk as fast as possible to get in and out of the shop. Sometimes there used to be a queue, or the papers had arrived late, so there would be half a dozen people standing in the shop just waiting for the local paper to come. I would be so anxious and silently crying because I knew they would be waiting until I left the shop before spilling out the next 'funny line' they had just thought of. The longer I was in the shop, the longer the time they had to come up with more abusive, offensive and mostly racist comments, with no thought to the fact I was just a skinny 12-year-old kid who didn't really have any understanding of how awful these things they were saying were. What I did know was it hurt, hurt so much, and it didn't feel good; I did understand the words they shouted were hateful, full of rage and anger.

So not only was my day-to-day school life just a breeding ground of abuse and racist bullying, but also my daily newspaper pick up after school would just be more of the same. Sometimes I would hide behind the library for a few minutes and watch these gangs on the benches. Then, if someone new came to join the group, I would very quickly run to the shop as fast as I could as they were distracted by someone blocking the view to the entrance of the newsagents and run back out as fast as I could. Just two shops away from the newsagents was an alleyway, this led to the back of the shops and a stairwell to the flats above. So, upon approaching the precinct, if I saw a big gang of people on these benches, I would walk all of the way around to the back of the shops by the park behind it and go up the back of this alleyway. This meant I only had to walk the length of two shops in front of them to get the paper; this reduced a couple of minutes off the time I would be paraded within their eye line. However, this also meant that I took a few minutes longer returning home, to which I would face the wrath of my mum.

"Where have you been?" she would say as soon as I walked through the door. "What took you so long? I told you to go straight there and straight back" was some of the things my mum would retort.

"Nowhere", I would say, of course, I couldn't tell them the real reason because I knew I would just get a 'don't be stupid' response.

She didn't understand, as it never happened when we went to the shops together. There was another newsagent at the top of the estate, which was about half a mile away, so sometimes if there were too many people around the benches and around the bottom shops, I would run to the very, very top of the estate to get the paper there, as there were no places where people could just hang out outside that newsagent, but it would take so much longer. So, I had to pretend many times that the papers were late arriving and I had to wait for them even though my mom was still angry. I wouldn't get away with it often as they would see other people in the streets coming back with a paper under their arm, but even my mom being angry for me taking so long was much better than having to walk back past these gangs on the benches. There was a chip shop just next door to the newsagents; sometimes, when these bully boys didn't get enough satisfaction from just name-calling, they would just throw the bags of chips over me or the batter bits like I was a target at a funfair. I could do nothing to defend myself. My dad used to do the football pools every week; and if he missed the scores on the telly I would have to go and buy 'the pink', a small newspaper dedicated to the sport, this was delivered separately from the newspaper, leading to double the trauma.

Racist abuse towards me wasn't just contained at school or groups of people gathered in gangs around the shops. It would be on the walk to school, the walk up the street, the walk along the roads to go to the shops. People would just shout things out their car windows as they sped by.

"PAKI!"

"FUCK OFF BACK TO WHERE YOU CAME FROM"

"WHAT'S FOR TEA? CURRY?" strangers would shout out their windows.

I assumed most of these people were adults; otherwise, they wouldn't be driving. So, I would just keep my head down and look at the footpath in front of me. How could these people who had never seen me before and know nothing about me shout at me in the street or throw cans? I was a 12-year-old girl and didn't understand at all. But what I did know was it wasn't nice; it was horrible; it made me feel like I was the most hated person in the world. A small part of me blamed my parents for making me wear that coat that was too big, or purple tights under my school uniform. It had to be someone else's fault because I hadn't done anything wrong. All I know is that people didn't like me. This led me to not wanting to do as I was told at home so much. Why should I tidy my room? Why should I dust? Why should I clean out the fire grate? When it's their fault I was being abused, it was their fault we were poor and couldn't afford to look nice; like some of the other kids, I couldn't afford to have the best games for people to want to play with me. I couldn't afford the trendy uniform that seemed to make other people at school likeable; if I had all of these things, it would distract from the colour of my skin, which was something none of us could change. If I could have taken one pill or magic drink that would take this colour away, then my God, I would have had a gallon of it.

My Dad was working full time, which meant my mum was at home most days, so most nights, my mom would be out either seeing friends, relatives or going to bingo, occasionally, my dad would have to pick my mom up from bingo, leaving me looked after for half an hour by my sister. There were nine years between us, we didn't have much in common, we would rarely spend time together. But I do recall my mom loved talcum powder, there were always footprints of Imperial Leather talc on the bathroom floor after a bath, which smelt lovely.
So, one evening my sister went messing around in our parent's bedroom, she called me upstairs and started throwing talcum powder on me, I didn't like it as I knew we would get into trouble, so I was trying to stomp the talcum powder into the carpet as it fell on the floor, she must have emptied whole bottle of imperial leather talc all over me, my hair was grey, my clothes stank and I looked like a ghost,

my sister found this highly amusing, until mum and Dad arrived back, we ran to our bedrooms and lay very quietly, although this didn't mask the smell of this talcum powder all over the house.

"They've been messing", I heard my mom say, then we listened to the footsteps on the stairs.

But, of course, we hadn't cleaned up correctly, so the evidence was everywhere; once my mom switched the bedroom light on and saw the state I was in, covered head to foot in talcum powder, she instantly said (although evident).

"Have you been messing about with my talc?"

"No", of course, I would say while standing there covered in talc, but I didn't want to be the one in trouble.

"It was Carole."

Mom proceeded to Carole's bedroom and asked. "Have you been messing with my talc?"

"No", replied Carole.

To which I pleaded, "Yes, she has."

"What have you done to your sister?" my mom said.

"I'm trying to make her white," said Carole.

"What?" replied my mom.

Carole started crying; I was told to get to my room. My mom, my dad, and Carole were now downstairs, and all I could hear my mom saying was, "I'm going up the school."

Why would my mum go up the school because my sister put talcum powder all over me? But, of course, I didn't understand; I was just happy that I wasn't the one in trouble because I hadn't done anything wrong.

I remember seeing my mum sewing my sister's school shirt the following day, but I thought nothing of it. Some kids were asking why they saw my mom in school. "I don't know", I would reply because I didn't know.

It wasn't until years later that I learned that my sister, too, was being bullied, in fights and being called a Paki lover just because she was my sister. Hence, her reasoning for covering me in talcum powder was to remove my colour and stop the bullying.

The mid-80s was when many comedies on the telly sitcoms like Rising Damp, Bless This House, Mind Your Language, In Sickness and in Health, to name a few. Plus, some of the soaps like Coronation Street and Emmerdale Farm would make many references to the 'Paki shop' and racist comments about the 'coons' next-door going home and calling people of colour 'terrorists. In response to news reports of fighting, riots and social unrest at the time, people were often heard saying things such as 'it's always the dirty stinking Pakis' and 'the blacks why don't they all just fuck off back home back to where they come from' or 'coming here in boat loads' would be aired of people commenting. Even TV shows like the Royal Variety or game shows where they have a comedian on stage many of them would be making jokes, racist jokes or putting on Indian accents as a subject of what they thought was a funny joke usually to find that the audience was roaring with laughter.

I was now starting to understand what Paki meant and what this colour denotes to other people. According to these shows that are always on prime-time TV, I'm one of those dirty stinking Pakis. I'm one of those people they're wanting to get sent home, I am one of those people they think came on a boat, I'm one of those people that are attempting to infect their country, trying to take over their land, I'm one of these people that do all the dirty jobs. I'm one of those people no one wants to be friends with or talk to or be seen with as if they too would be bullied or frozen out of their circle and disliked. These people targeted on the news look like me!!!!!

Oh my God, I am a Paki!!!!

CHAPTER SEVEN

Hanging on the telephone

Early teenage years had me and the girl who pushed her chair out in that very first class of high school becoming friends. Her name was Jane, I would walk up to her house just a few streets away from where I lived, and we would sit in her bedroom playing 'Kerplunk', which was a game I really wanted, but my parents couldn't afford. Her family made me feel very welcome, almost like they didn't realise I was different. This was an incredible feeling. My new friend Jane and I would have such a laugh together, finally, finally, I had someone in my life who was not bothered by anything anyone else said so for those few hours I was allowed up to her house were terrific, it was the best feeling ever. Until Jane introduced me to her neighbour Debbie Hinton. Debbie and Jane had been neighbours since they were born, which led them to be best friends and grow up together.

"This is Susan, my friend from school," Jane introduced me to Debbie. Debbie was a year older than us and went to a different school. Debbie just stared at me and went back into the house. We didn't think much of it as we would usually just sit on her garden wall, occasionally chatting to the rest of her friends, both boys and girls who lived in the same street as her.

A few times, Jane and I used to spend time together either at her house or occasionally, she would come down to mine, and we would sit in my bedroom and talk about boys and pop stars and just do things that young girls do. I preferred to go up to Jane's house as her house was much nicer, and she had plenty of games and all the things that I didn't have, which made me a little jealous. However, Jane was happy to share. A couple of times, Debbie would come out and sit with us for a very short time and always go in or be called in by her mum. However, there were other people in the street too, Michael Kylie, Keith Jones, and Adrian Rathbone would stop by and have a little chat, and everything was fine; finally, I had friends, and it felt great. Until a few times, when I would go up to see Jane.

"I can't come out. I'm playing with Debbie," she would say, meaning she was only playing with Debbie that day and not me.

Sometimes Jane would go back into her house, and I would hear her telling Debbie that I was at the door, to which Debbie would say "If you're playing with her, or if she's coming in, I'm going home."

Debbie didn't like me, and I understood they had both been friends a long time before I was on the scene. Debbie wanted Jane to herself. No, no, surely not my Jane, My only friend Jane. I'm happy to share, although really, I didn't want to because Jane was slightly different when Debbie was around. One day, the three of us, were sitting on Debbie's garden wall. Within minutes Debbie's mum opened the door calling for Debbie to go in. Debbie instantly stood up and went into the house, which we heard her mum saying.

"I've told you about mixing with her."

"What?" I thought Jane and Debbie had been friends for years, forever it seemed, why would her mum say that. Jane looked embarrassed. Debbie's mum flung the door open again, shouting, "And you can get off my wall."

"We are just sitting here," replied Jane, confused.

"Get off my wall", Debbie's mom repeated.

So, we moved, Jane went really quiet,

"I better go in," she said.

And I went home.

The next day at school, I asked Jane. "When are we playing out next?" "I don't know." she'd reply.

"I'm with Debbie this weekend", she continued.

So confused after the events of the previous weekend, I would say. "Oh, can't I play?"

"No." she would reply ", Debbie doesn't like you."

"I'm not trying to take you away from her," I said, thinking Debbie may want Jane to herself, as they were friends first.

"I know." Jane said. "But her mum won't let us play if I'm with you."

Then it dawned on me once again, the colour of my skin was not only making it difficult for me to have friends, but now it was ruining my friend's relationships too. I seemed even if I could find someone to be my friend they couldn't because they would lose their other friends, and I wasn't enough on my own. I just wasn't enough full stop.

"Can't we all just be friends?" I would plead to Jane.

"I was Debbie's friend first," Jane replied.

"But we can still be friends at school," she said, trying to salvage my feelings.

“Ok,” I said, defeated.

I now had a couple of friends in school, by ‘friends’, I mean people that would allow me to sit next to them in class or even at lunchtimes, but whose family wouldn’t let me see them at home or have me in their house. Even Tracey, whose mum called me a wog, became a friend at school. It wasn’t Tracy’s fault that her mum didn’t like me, so sometimes Tracey would lie to her mum and pretend she was going to see a different friend and, she would come down to my house. I was her secret friend; I accepted this. It was better than nothing.

Jane’s family were great; they accepted me, but I couldn’t see Jane as much as I wanted to. When I asked her; the reply would often be that Debbie asked me first. So very occasionally, when Debbie was busy, Jane and I would get together and walk the streets for miles out of the estate so no one would see us together and report back to Debbie. So, I didn’t see Jane as much as I liked, but we had such a laugh when we did get together and I was just grateful for that.

We were now of an age where we started noticing boys; we basically fancied everyone, it seemed no boys were interested in me. It was one thing having so-called friends, but for them to actually desire someone who looked so different and who no one liked because of how they looked, that was never going to happen.

On the days that Debbie was away or not allowed out, Jane and I would sit on a wall behind the hedge, so Debbie couldn’t see us. Some of the other people in the street would still stop by and talk, and there was one boy in particular called Keith Jones who was very good looking; all the girls fancied him, but I used to help him with his homework because I was so clever at school. I helped him a few times and even did homework for him mainly because I tried to make people like me, but I knew he wasn’t interested in me romantically.

Then I got into my very first fight at school.

Everyone always knew who fancied who at school; people would always be teased, or you'd see names written on school desks. Then one day in the PE changing rooms, after being subjected to the usual abuse, which I would ignore and ignore and ignore time after time. Nicola Weston, one of the popular girls, started taunting me more and more, mainly to show off. Everyone laughed, and the more everyone laughed, the more things she would say to me. I would just pretend I didn't hear her and carry on getting changed as fast as possible. Unbeknown to me, Nicola had a thing for Keith Jones.

"Keep away from Keith Jones; he's not going to fancy you", she would say. "I don't fancy him", I would reply.

"Yes, you do, you are all over him, he doesn't fancy Pakis, leave him alone", she shouted across the changing room.

I don't know what changed to this day, but I knew I was fed up with the constant abuse and torment, and the fact that I answered back enraged Nicola and the jeering crowd behind her, she came right up to my face nose to nose saying, "Yes, you do, you are doing his homework for him," she said.

"I don't fancy him", I would reply.

"No one would fancy you, you're ugly, and you are a Paki, you smell, why don't you fuck off back home", she replied while spitting in my face.

People were laughing behind her, she continued. "No one wants you here, so stay away from our boys."

"We are just friends." I would say.

Everyone just started jeering.

"Paki, Paki, Paki!"

I was backed into the corner of the changing room. I couldn't get around the crowd or go through them and certainly couldn't get past Nicola, who was pushing me into the corner, egged on by her friends, pushing, pushing, pushing at me, and I couldn't put my shirt on and dropped my bag.

"JUST FUCK OFF" I shouted.

Where did that come from? I thought, it was as though I had no control over my mouth and it just fell out, now to suffer the consequences. Everyone jeered as though I dared to get angry.

"What did you say?" Nicola asked.

"Say it to my face," she said whilst pushing in her nose almost to mine. "What did you say? What did you say? Say it again? She continued.

I really don't know what happened to me that day, but I just shouted, "FUCK OFF BITCH!"

Nicola instantly slapped me across the face, making me fall onto the bench beside us. Something inside of me just snapped to make me jump up and slap her back. She grabbed my hair, and we were grappling on the floor; everyone was shouting.

"Punch her, Nicola!"

The teachers came in and pulled us apart.

Breathless and with tufts of my hair still in her hand, Nicola pleaded with the teachers, "It wasn't me, she started it" with an accusatory finger pointed at me.

"No, I didn't", I would retort.

Finally, the bell rang for the next lesson, and the teachers just told us to get to class. All I heard was the whispers, 'Nicola beat Susan up' the rest of that day, which made her popularity escalate even higher.

I don't know what came over me to actually fight back for the first time ever, not just with words but physically too. I didn't like this feeling, it didn't make me feel better, and I certainly had no intention of doing it again. Usually, when you hear of stories about bullying and somebody fights back, that's usually the end of it. However, in my case, it ended up being more of a challenge for others, as other people now wanted to fight me, so they also had the attention Nicola had that day. The bullying and abuse escalated with the sole purpose for them to say 'wait until you get to the gates.'

"Louise just offered out Susan", I would hear people say so often; this meant a challenge to a fight. So many people would gather and hang around by the school gates each day; the teachers often had to walk me out. Sometimes I would just stay back at school hiding in the toilets until they all disappeared, even though doing that meant me being in trouble at home for being so late from school. But I would rather get shouted out by my mom than be beaten up every day after school for nothing. Even the people I thought were my friends, Jane and Tracy didn't want to be involved and were nowhere to be seen when I had to walk out the gates. I can't stand much more of this; I hate school, everyone hates me, and there was nothing I could do about it. I tried telling my mom many times.

"Everyone keeps calling me a Paki at school", I complained.

"Just ignore them", she would say. Of course, that was the automatic response every time or "take no notice."

Then it changed to, "you're not a Paki anyway." my mom would say. "But I am." I would reply.

"You're not a Paki." my mum would say "Pakis come from Pakistan; they don't know anything."

Mom didn't understand; these were the days when you were either black, white, or a Paki; there was nothing in between. So, if you had black skin, you were black; if you had white skin, you are white, but if you had brown skin, you are a Paki, that's it. So, it didn't matter what your origins were if your skin was brown, you were a Paki....nothing else came into it.

When you're a child, you believe everything that your parents tell you. "I am not a Paki, I am not a Paki, I am not a Paki" was constantly going round and round in my head. So, feeling a little braver, whenever people started calling me names, I would respond with "I'm not a Paki."

"Yes, you are", they would reply, and that would make them just start chanting, "Paki, Paki, Paki!"

"I am not a Paki", I would shout back as if I hoped that they would believe me, but it was just adding fuel to the fire.

Every time somebody said something within the school, that would be my automatic reply, "I am not a Paki." I don't know why I bothered, as it didn't stop anything. Even going to pick up the daily newspaper. I had to just take the name-calling and abuse as I certainly couldn't respond back to any of those big boys, and I definitely didn't want to be beaten up by any of them for attempting to do so.

Queuing for school dinners was always a nightmare, everyone looking at what everybody else was having, and all the people who were friends would all eat the same thing. One day, curry was one of the choices on the menu. Now, of course, I knew that curry is one thing that Asians eat, so I definitely would not have that. If I didn't have curry, they might believe I'm not a Paki. So, of course, as it was my turn to ask for food, everyone's eyes were on me, waiting to see what I chose, and I decided on pie, which was something that tasted awful at school, but I didn't care. As soon as I made my choice, everyone around me started saying:

"Aren't you having the Curry Susan? Why don't you have a Curry Susan? Why don't you want Curry?"

I just ignored them, hoping that this would make them realise that I couldn't really be a Paki; otherwise, I would definitely have chosen the Curry. But this didn't work, it confused them, and so instead, they started throwing Curry at me with their spoons. I'd hear people shouting," is there any Curry left for Susan Sir?" to which everyone would titter.

However, people were surprised that Curry wasn't my choice of dinner, and it made some people go quiet in their confusion. I can only imagine how worse things would be if I had actually had the Curry; it would just confirm everything they thought to be true. I would have smelt of spice on my breath, and so people that weren't in the dining hall would smell that and again confirm everything they thought they knew, so that was it that was the day I made the decision to never have a Curry for the rest of my life. I felt so alone. No one understood me, even I don't understand.

Sometimes Jane's mum and dad would go out of an evening, leaving Jane, who was an only child on her own, so I would go up to her house, and we do our usual things, talking about Top of the Pops, talking about boys, hair, makeup everything girls chat about. And then we discovered chat lines.

Chat lines were the best thing ever. Jane's house had a landline, something we did not have at home, and we would find these chat line numbers in the back of our magazines, and we would call them up. We thought it was the best thing, talking to complete strangers and being rude and funny and just having a laugh. Hours we would be on these chat lines, hours and hours, we loved the attention, it was like a party on the phone, these boys that sounded really fit. We could be anyone we wanted to be, and it was great. So, we started calling these empty voices on the other line our boyfriends. We would sit on her stairs in the hallway, where the telephone was located, holding the handset between our ears and just talking gibberish and being cheeky for hours. No one could tell that we were only almost 14 years old. These boys on either end of the phone sounded much older; it made us feel great having the attention of the older boys.

Every single time her mom and dad went out, even if it was to go shopping for an hour or two hours, we would instantly be on the phone, sometimes one of us would keep a lookout outside, waiting for her mom and dad's car to come back, and we put the phone down very quickly. This went on for a couple of weeks, so we started writing these boys names on our school books and on the desks at school, and we talked about them like they were boyfriends to others, and no one would believe we had boyfriends, as they were older than us. We were having the time of our lives, and it felt great.

Over that phone, I was just a voice; they couldn't see me, so to people on the other end of the phone, I was just an ordinary girl. But we were having such fun, we were very naïve back then, as we would paint a picture in our heads of what they looked like, and we thought they were around 17 years old, which to us seemed really old. We had no idea at the time that we were probably speaking to people in their 40s, with beer bellies and beards, and the extreme to what we thought was true. Over that phone I had a 'boyfriend' who was a boy called Paul, and he lived in London, he had his own business, made lots of money and was very funny and had blonde hair, so, of course, I instantly thought he looked like Billy Idol. This was great; now Jane and I shared a secret that no one else had, we had secret boyfriends, and it really bonded us. Until her mom and dad came banging on my front door.

"We need to speak to you about Jane and Susan," said Janes mom sharply.

"What?" my mum would say, letting them in the door.

"This!" Jane's mom said, thrusting a piece of paper into my mom's hand.

"382 pounds!" she screamed at my mom,

"What! My mom just looked at me in anger.

It was a phone bill. £392 in today's money is over £2000.

"They have been calling chat lines behind our backs" Janes mom was so angry.

My mum looked at me as though I were about to turn into stone. Jane and I didn't even give a thought about the fact that these super long telephone calls to our secret boyfriends cost any money, let alone be so expensive, my mum and dad could never afford to pay that.

And that was it. Jane and I were banned from seeing each other. My only friend in the whole wide world, the only bit of enjoyment I have in my life had now been taken away.
My life was over.

CHAPTER EIGHT

Dangerous Liaisons

I felt I had no place to breathe. I felt like I was in a dark room sitting in a corner, hugging my knees all of the time. My parents were super strict; they were old school, sometimes, my mom, in particular, took things too far. One day, I accidentally knocked over my mom's cup of coffee, which was on the floor by where she sat, her slipper came off instantly, and I was smacked so hard, no matter how I pleaded, even though I would be crying so hard.

"What you crying for?" She would shout.

"Stop crying, or I will give you something to cry for." She would bellow.

This never worked; being told to stop crying while smacked with a slipper never worked.

We had no central heating in our house, and as bath time was only allowed on a Sunday as that was when we could afford to put the immersion heater on, by putting 50 pence's into the electric heater under the stairs to heat the water. So, we would have to have daily 'strip washes' in the kitchen sink. I hated this; it was so cold to be standing naked in a kitchen in the harsh winter times of the mid-80s. We had to wash with the water boiled in a saucepan, so I would wash as fast as I could, so I could run back into the living room by the then newly installed gas heater from the council. This was an upgrade from the coal fire, but we were only allowed to have one panel on at a time. One day my mother thought I washed too quickly,

"You haven't had time for a wash", she would say.

"Yes, I have", I replied.

"No, you haven't, the towel is not even that wet," said mom.

"But it's cold", I would plead.

"You don't know the meaning of the word cold" mom said.

It was with that she stripped off my clothes and threw me into the back garden, in the snow, and the pouring rain, naked, to prove what cold really meant. As we lived in a mid-terraced house, people in the homes on either side of us could see clearly into our back garden. So, I stood there naked, trying to conceal myself, freezing cold, and crying to be let back in, I had no idea what the neighbours thought, and my mom didn't seem to care; she was trying to prove a point after all.

My mom was always trying to prove points, as everyone had to have a bath on the same day, that being a Sunday, sometimes we had to share bathwater, which thinking about it now was disgusting. Still, at the time, it was all we could afford, and we were unaware of how dirty it was to step into someone else's dirty bathwater, but we had no choice. So my mom used to wash my hair in the bath, we had no shower, not even an attachment on the taps at this point, so it was with a jug in the bathwater that my hair would be washed. Mom was always in a hurry, as she was going to bingo most nights, so her washing my hair meant jugs of water just being thrown over my head and rubbing my scalp so vigorously until my head was stinging from the scratches of her nails. The water would go over my face most of the time, without warning. I didn't have time to hold my breath, causing me to start coughing and spluttering as soapy water would go up into my nose and into my eyes.

"Stop it!" she would scream at me.

"It's going in my eyes and mouth", I would splutter.

"It won't hurt you", mom would say.

"It's only water."

But of course, I couldn't stop myself from choking every time this water would go up my nose or in my mouth, to which point my mom would pull me backwards by my hair and hold me under the water, to prove to me that water doesn't hurt. I would be screaming and fighting to get out from beneath the water, but the more I screamed and fought, the longer she would hold my head under the water. One time I was screaming so loud for so long that my dad shouted up the stairs.

"That's enough!" he shouted.

"She is scared of a little bit of water!" mom would say.

Why does my mom hate me so much? I'd never heard Carole, my sister, getting the same treatment; in fact, my sister and I were treated entirely differently. Is this because she was her own child? And the bond was different? She loved her more, clearly.

Another time I remember squealing in my bedroom because there was a massive spider on the wall.

"Mom, can you come and get the spider out of my bedroom, please?"

"They won't hurt you", she would say. "Stop being a big baby."

I would be sobbing my heart out; I couldn't get to sleep in fear this giant spider would eat me alive.

"Stop crying", she would shout, "you're bigger than him" that didn't help at all.

At this point, my mom told me to come downstairs, where she pulled me by my arm into the back garden and locked me in the coal shed. The coal shed was precisely that, it was a cold brick building in the garden, with a small broken window boarded up, and it was where we kept the coal from when we had a coal fire, it was dirty and dark and damp and must have been full of spiders. She threw me in there and locked the door with the key to try and teach me that spiders won't hurt me. I screamed and cried so hard and so much until my throat was red raw; the whole estate must have heard me. There were substantial scratch marks on the coal house door from me trying to escape and fight to get out. This was not a way to teach children that spiders and creepy crawlies don't hurt; in fact, it might make it much worse. To this day if I see even the smallest of spiders I instantly freeze and my anxiety takes over. I even slept in my car one night a few years ago, when I opened the front door to my house, and there was a massive spider in the hallway. I do not have many nightmares these days, but the ones I do have, most of the time, are about spiders and people not realising just how afraid I am of them and throwing one at me, thinking it's funny.

Mom had always been too strict, where had the kind hearted loving foster mother who just wanted to love all the babies gone? Why was she now so cruel? Was it because babies are easier to control? But early teenagers were more difficult to manage? I wasn't a naughty child, I dare not be, I was too scared of my mom. So, maybe she was getting fed up of the extra trouble she had to deal with, like the bullying and sly comments people made, maybe she realised her sister was right when she told her 'It would be nothing but trouble having me'. So, in turn I think mom must have been 'taking out her frustrations on me' who knows?

Why was my mum so angry at me all of the time? I don't ever remember these things happening to my sister; why did they love her more than me? It must be because she's their own child, or was it because she was white? Or was it because they were also being abused for having me in their life too? I don't know, and I couldn't work it out. I was just a 14-year-old child, without any escape from hatred. I would go to school and constantly be tormented and bullied, outdoors going to the shops, and I would be taunted and ridiculed, and at home, I felt I was hated, not wanted and unloved. The only tiny bit of a break I had was the short time I had with my friend Jane. Now we were banned from seeing each other. I had nothing; I hated my life. I had no escape. I had no rest from all of this sadness. I had to get away, I had to get away from everyone and everything, anywhere, anything was better than this. I didn't want to live anymore. I certainly didn't want to live this life I was living. I had to get away. I had to run away.

I had no money, friends, or anything, so how could I get away? I was 14. I thought I knew everything, I thought I could rule the world in my head, but the reality was I knew nothing and no one and had nothing or anyone.

No one, except my secret boyfriend on the chat lines.

There was a phone box at the end of our street, so, when I went over to the shops for my mom, I took some of the small coins from my mom's change and went to the telephone box to call Paul. It had been a few weeks since we spoke, but he remembered me; I told him I had no money, so he asked the telephone number for the phone box, and call me straight back, which he did; I told him how unhappy I was. He seemed to really care. It was so good to hear someone care about my feelings.

"Don't worry, I will look after you", he would say.

"Just leave; you can come and live with me," he said.

Oh my God, I had somewhere I could go and someone who cared about me; this was the answer to all my prayers and a way to escape from my life. Yes, I must, I can't carry on like this, but how was I going to get out of the house with a bag full of clothes.

My sister was in her mid-20s at this point, and she used to stop out very late at night at the local Rollerdrome in town. She was coming home at 3 or 4 o'clock in the morning most nights, much to my parent's anger. "Using this house like a hotel", I would hear them argue.

So, sometimes my sister would sneak around the back of the house where my bedroom was and throw small stones at my window in the middle of the night, in a bid to get me to wake up and very quietly open the front door, to let her in without mum and dad knowing. This happened many times. I was fed up with my mom being angry with me for no reason most days. So, I deliberately made a noise on the stairs when letting my sister in, during the early hours of the morning, so it woke my mom, and then Carole got in trouble. I revelled in the fact that she was the one they were angry at just for those few hours and not me.

That's it! That's what I'll do! I will wait until the middle of the night and sneak downstairs to leave the house, and they won't know anything until they get up, that will give me a few hours head start, and I could be in London with Paul by then I thought. And that's precisely what I did; I packed a few clothes, took my mom's makeup bag and some change off the mantle-piece, and walked out of the house at 5:00 o'clock in the morning, knowing that once that door clicked shut, there was no going back. I went to the phone box at the end of the street and called Paul.

"I've done it, I've done it! I'm out of the house, I've left, please come and get me," I said nervously.

Paul responded with, "I am working at the moment; I have one more job to do."

I didn't really know what he did for a job, but he said "If you jump on the bus to Birmingham, I will pick you up from there and take you to my house."

"OK, that's fine, I can do that," I said.

I knew where the bus station was because my mom and I used to go to town to get the shopping.

We had never seen a picture of each other, so he didn't know what I looked like, which I thought was a blessing, and I didn't know what he looked like either. I wanted to make sure I looked nice, so armed with my mom's makeup bag, I went to the public toilets over the precinct and put on lipstick and eye-liner to try to make myself look 18, and so no one would wonder why there was a young girl on her own on the bus. So, I plastered my face in makeup and then waited and waited for the first bus to Birmingham to arrive.

Upon reaching the end of the line in Birmingham, I went to the nearest phone box and called Paul, who then called me back, and we arranged for him to come and pick me up. I hadn't been to Birmingham before; it felt so big, the huge buildings were much more significant and many more people than Wolverhampton. I felt like a little girl lost in a big city waiting to start her brand-new adult life. However, I was also terrified. So, I just stayed exactly where I was and, I didn't move anywhere, and just waited and waited for Paul to come and get me.

It was late afternoon before Paul came; I told him what I was wearing and where I was standing and just waited for him to pull up. A car pulled in front of me, and there was a man with shoulder-length curly blonde hair driving, who looked about 40 years old; he sat there for a while just staring, and then he got out of the car and walked over to me, he was pretty short, wore glasses and wasn't attractive at all.

"Are you Susan?" he said.

"Yes," I replied nervously, "are you, Paul?"

"Yes, come and get in the car," he said.

This wasn't Paul, the secret boyfriend that I imagined; he looked nothing like Billy Idol. Billy Idol was half his age and way better looking.

"I haven't got long, got a couple more jobs to go to," he said, whisking me into the car.

What could I do now? I knew nothing else; I wasn't old enough or tough enough to tell him I didn't want to go. I just couldn't go back home and face the anger the parents would have from me doing this. So, I had no choice; I just sat in the back of the car. I just had to do what he told me to do.

"I've just got to go and pick a friend up and do a job, then I'll take you to mine," he said.

I was so excited to see what London was going to be like, you see it on the TV and in films, I was now going to be an adult, I didn't need anyone else, this was my new life, despite Paul not being the person I thought he was, he was still saving me from my awful, awful life. So, I just sat quietly in the back of the car with my bag beside me. We drove for what seemed like a few hours and then pulled up outside a house, and he went inside, leaving me in the car; he then returned with this really pretty, skinny, blonde, white girl.

"This is Susan," he said.

She got in the car.

"This is Rachel." He said.

"Hello," I said nervously, thinking to myself has he got another girlfriend?

She was lovely, she was so pretty, and had a huge smile and big sparkling eyes. We pulled up outside of a pub, and Paul went inside. Rachel turned to talk to me; she was very friendly.
"Where are you from?" she asked.

"Wolverhampton," I said.

"How did you meet Paul?" she questioned.
"Oh, we've been talking for a while," I said.
Why did she ask that? Please don't be jealous of me, you've got nothing to be jealous of, I'm nowhere near as pretty and bubbly and friendly and lovely as you are I thought, please don't hate me, I can't go back to my life. Paul returned to the car and opened the door to let Rachel out,

"Are you ready?" he asked Rachel.

"Yes," she replied;

He then opened the door for me to get out, and I just followed them into the pub. Wow, I loved my new adult life, going to a pub, like an adult, and nobody blinking an eyelid. The pub was full of smoke and full of men. I just stood as close I could get to Paul, and Rachel walked off in front, and all the men just started cheering and laughing and raising their glasses as they burst into a song.

"Happy birthday to you, happy birthday to you", they all started singing really loudly.

Rachel walked towards a man sitting down on a chair, she took her coat off, and Paul began to play some music, everyone was cheering and singing Happy Birthday and laughing, and it was so noisy. I had no idea what was happening, but Rachel started taking her clothes off in the middle of the room and in front of everyone! Under her oversized coat, she had white stockings, suspenders and a matching bra with the highest heels I've ever seen. She had a huge smile and started sitting on this man's lap and singing to him, she then started walking around the boys, and she continued to take her bra off and swing it around her head before returning to sit on a gentlemen's lap. I don't think I blinked the whole time, so this is what a kissogram is? I didn't even know what I felt as I'd never seen anything like that before. Fifteen minutes later, we were back in the car and onto another pub. Rachel was sitting in the front seat, trying to put her clothes back on. "What did you think?" she turned to ask me.

I was just flabbergasted,

"That was amazing," was all I could think of saying.

How she just stood in the middle of a pub full of men and took her clothes off smiling, and everyone loved her. At that moment, she was the centre of attention, and she had a big smile on her face all the way through.

"You were fantastic," I said.

"Thank you," she replied.

After a short journey in the car, we arrived at another venue, and precisely the same thing happened again, only this time there were girls there too, and no one looked at her strangely or judged her or anything. People just enjoyed what she did, and she too seemed to enjoy what she did. We returned to the car where Paul gave her a wad of money, more money than I'd ever seen in my life, and then he dropped her home.

So, this is what London life is like; I couldn't have been more shocked, I'd never experienced anything like it before. I just thought that's how people lived in London, she turned to me before she went inside her house.

"Do you think you could do this?" she asked.
"I don't know, I'll try," I said.

"Great, I'll see you again", replied Rachel.
And with that, she went into the house.
Paul just turned and said "I'll take you to my house now; what did you think of that?"

I replied "It was great, she is so lovely."

After about half an hour of driving, we pulled up at Paul's place; it wasn't anything special. As we walked into the living room, there just seemed to be clutter everywhere.

"Do you want to drink?" he asked,

"No, thank you," I replied; my mom told me to always politely refuse anyone offering you anything.

So, we sat and chatted for a while, and I told him about what home life was like, and the bullying I got at school etc.

"How old are you?" he asked.

"14", I replied.

"Where are you from?"

"Wolverhampton", I answered.

"No, where are you really from?"

"Wednesfield."

I didn't know what he really meant, but I think he meant because of the colour of my skin.

"You best get some sleep; you can sleep on the sofa; I need to go to bed," he said.

And with that, I just lay down on the sofa until the morning, not really knowing what the new day would bring. I don't think I got much sleep; I was in a strange house with someone I didn't really know, I was scared, really scared. Paul got up quite early despite us only going to bed in the early hours.

"I've got work to do, but I'll drop you in town". He said.

"What?" I replied, "How can you drop me in the middle of a big city? To do what? To go where? I've got nowhere to go?" I said.

"I'll drop you at the police station. Then, they'll take you home," he said.

I couldn't go home. He didn't understand how much is that was the absolute last place I could go, especially now, I definitely could not go home.

"OK," I said.

How had everything changed? It seemed as soon as he knew my age and that I wasn't wholly English, he was no longer the friendly, supportive secret boyfriend I thought I had, and he was no longer my saviour anymore. And that's precisely what he did, he dropped me outside the police station, with my bag.

"Just tell them your parents have kicked you out", and he sped off. After that, I never saw or heard from him again... Well, that was until many years later when I saw a picture of him in the newspaper with a story of him being sentenced to 12 years in prison for the rape and grooming of young girls.

update
In 1994 Paul Doyle was cleared of raping a 23-year-old woman.
June 1998 Paul Doyle was convicted of raping a 18-year-old woman, indecently assaulting a 19-year-old girl and 2 charges of indecent assault of a 15-year-old girl.

He was sentenced to 12 years in prison.

CHAPTER NINE

There's something about Mary

I didn't know what to do, I knew no one, I had no money, I had no place to go, I had no friends, but anything was better than going home, going back to school, and being bullied every day. I didn't know what to do. If I walked into that police station and told them I was only 14, they would most certainly take me back home. I couldn't imagine how much my mom would beat me after this.

So, I took a deep breath, walked into the police station, to the reception and said "My mom's kicked me out, and I've got nowhere to go."

"How old are you?" they asked.

"16", I replied, thinking I must look 16 with my mom's makeup still all over my face."

"And you definitely can't go home?" they queried again.

"No, I can't go home," I replied.

"Why did they throw you out?" they asked.

"I don't know; she didn't like me," I replied.

"OK, take a seat," they said.

I sat there for almost two hours, at this police station in London, were they going to call my parents? Will they send me to prison? I felt numb and scared, should I just run out the door?

"OK, we have found somewhere for you to go," said the policeman. Oh my God, I thought I really didn't have to go home.

"We have found out a hostel for you to stay."

Wow, I'd never been to a hostel before, this was going to be great living in a hotel, I'd never stayed in a hotel before. At this point I didn't know the difference between a hostel and a hotel, so I sat in the back of the police car, I'd never been in a police car before so I was slightly excited but also anxious and scared. I was hoped this wasn't secretly going to take me to prison. Just 15 minutes later, we pulled up outside this vast house, and I walked inside.

"This is Susan, she's 16, and her mum has kicked her out," the policeman said to the nun who opened the door.

"Oh, hello Susan, how are you?" she said.

"I'm fine, thank you."

Oh my God, they have brought me to a church. I'm going to be a nun, I thought.

"Let me show you to your room." the nun said.

"Take care of yourself," said the policeman, waving bye.

"Thank you", I shouted; basically, I was thanking him for not finding out I was actually 14.

The nun showed me upstairs to a room with a bed, and another girl was in there.

“This is Mary,” said the nun.

“Hello,” Mary said with a big friendly face; she was beautiful; she had bright red spiky hair, big black eye-liner, and black lips Just like Mary the punk that was on EastEnders at the time.

“I’ll leave you two together,” said the nun.

“How are you? What’s your name?” asked Mary.

“You will be fine here; I will look after you,” she said.

Really? I thought, have I got a new friend? She didn’t look at me strangely; she was friendly, and polite plus she wanted to help me.

“I’m OK, my mum kicked me out,” I said as we continued to chat when I told her I wanted my hair like hers.

She said, “I’ll do that for you.”

Oh, fabulous, I thought my new life was going to be the best. I never had someone wanting to do something lovely for me before. Mary and I were now friends; this was great, so we chatted late into the night.

“I’ve never been to London before; it’s so big,” I confessed.

“Yes, it is; I’ve never been either,” she replied.

“What do you mean?” I said, “We are in London.”

“No,” Mary laughed,

"Do you think we're in London now?"

"Yes," I replied.

"Oh Susan, you really are naïve; we're in Moseley," she giggled.

"Where's that?" I questioned.

"Birmingham," she said.

So, I just sat there confused, so I'd been in Birmingham all this time, and I thought I was in the bright lights of London.

"Oh no," I said, "I thought I was in London," and we both laughed for ages.

I was just so grateful that Mary not only was my new friend, but she also told me the truth, so that was it, we were immediately best friends, and because of that, I told her everything.

"So, you are really 14?" she asked upon me confessing all to my new friend.

"Yes, but please don't tell anyone, I can't go home."

"That's OK, you can trust me," Mary said.

All that week, Mary really looked out for me, many people were coming and going at the hostel, there was loud noises, people smoking and drinking at times, it was pretty scary.

Then Mary sat me down and said, "Your parents are going to be worried."

"No, they definitely are not," I said; "they hate me."

"You must call home and let them know you are OK."

"They won't care; they will be glad I've gone," I said, "plus we don't have a phone at home."

"Well, maybe write them a letter," Mary said.

"You don't understand Mary," I pleaded, "I have no one, they don't love me, I'm not even theirs, they're not my real mom and dad, people at school bully me and beat me up, I have no one, please don't tell anyone my real age."

"OK, OK," said Mary.

The following day Mary brought me downstairs to the communal area in the hostel, where there was the nun and a vicar. I walked in and just stared at Mary; I didn't know what was happening.

The vicar said, "Mary has told me everything."

I immediately burst into tears, "please don't send me home, please don't send me home," I was so scared.

"Don't worry," said the vicar, "I won't do that, but there is a service where we can let them know that you are OK, and we won't tell them where you are if you do not want us to."

"I don't want them to know anything, they don't care, they are better off without me, please, please don't tell them anything."

"No, no," said the vicar, "I promise you, we will not tell them, what happens is we get in touch with the local parish, and someone from there will go around the house to let your mom and dad know that you are well and OK, we will not send you home."

I was crying; I felt like I was gripping onto my new life by the very tips of my fingers.

"Please trust me," said the vicar, "we will not tell them where you are if you don't want to go home, you don't have to, but we have to let them know you are safe."

My whole bubble seemed to have burst, and I just stared at Mary. How could my brand-new friend betray me like this?

"I'm sorry," Mary said, "but it's the best thing."

"You promised," I said to her.

"You can write a note, and we can pass it on to your parents if you prefer," said the vicar.

"What could I possibly say to my mom and dad? They wouldn't understand anything, they wouldn't understand the reasons I left, why I couldn't be at home, why I couldn't go to school and why I had no friends.

"No, thank you," I said.

"OK," said the vicar, "we will just let them know that you have been found safe and well.

And off he went. Later that afternoon, the police and a social worker came to talk to me about why I had run away.

“You have to go home,” they said.

I was broken-hearted, now I was sobbing.

“Please don’t take me home, please don’t make me.”

“But your parents love you, the social worker said.

“No, they don’t, no one does.”

They didn’t get it. They didn’t understand.

“Well, you can’t stay here; you are only 14; we have to take you back to Wolverhampton,” they said.

“I would rather die than go home,” I replied.

The social worker went to a different room for a few minutes, and upon returning, they said “OK, we’re not going to take you home; if you’re adamant you don’t want to go, but we have to take you back to Wolverhampton, you cannot stay here, you are a minor.”

And with that, I was in the back of a car being brought back to Wolverhampton. My heart was pounding; what if we get all the way to Wolverhampton, and my mom and dad are just waiting there. I’m going to be beaten black and blue. As we turned up a really long drive towards a massive building in Wolverhampton, I questioned where we were.

“Are my mum and dad going to be here?”

“No, no, they’re not,” said the social worker; “This is Danescourt; you will be safe here.”

Danescourt was a children's home in Wolverhampton; I'd never heard of it before; it was in the posh part of Wolverhampton, well what I thought was the posh part. As we walked into this vast building, plenty of other children were playing pool and sitting around the place. It seemed OK, I was shown to my room and asked if I wanted something to eat, and I was introduced to a couple of the other children. Most of these children were older than me; they all seemed to be 16, 17 and 18. So, I just sat on a sofa on my own, and I was left there. I was just grateful my mum and dad were nowhere to be seen.

All the other kids looked really tough, and there would be swearing and smoking, and all kinds of things that I didn't do; it wasn't until later that day that I found out this it was almost like a holding children's home, it was where they put children whilst they were waiting to go to court for crimes, but I wasn't a naughty child, but I didn't really care where was, as long as I wasn't at home.

I remained in Danescourt for a few weeks, we had to have school lessons, and I was the brightest person in class as the lessons were for people much younger than the people in there. My parents had sent some clothes to last me for my duration in the home, and meetings were arranged by the social workers, between my parents and myself across a table, to discuss what had happened. I wasn't looking forward to seeing my parents again, I was just settled in Danescourt and was making friends, I didn't want anything to change.

"Why did you run away?" asked my mom.

"You are too strict," I would reply.

"Well, you shouldn't play up," said my mom, "and you took all my makeup."

I was flabbergasted; the main thing my mom was most concerned with was the fact that I took her makeup.

"Are you happy to go home?" asked the social worker.

"No, I don't want to go home," I replied.

"Stop being awkward," my mom would say, "and just come home."

But, I couldn't; I was scared to go home because I knew how much trouble I would be in and what I would get.

Over the next few weeks, my dad would write me letters telling me how things were at home, what he'd watched on the telly, and about Whiskey the cat. They would come to visit twice a week. I did notice that none of the other kids, to my knowledge, had parents visit them; this made me feel sorry for them. It also made me realise that my parents must have cared about me, to come and see me and make an effort. During one of the supervised visits, my mom and dad said things would change, and things would be different. They asked me if there was anything I wanted to do.

"I want to learn ballet," I said.

"Well, you're always walking on your tippy-toes," said my mom.

"Why don't you learn the piano?" said my dad.

"I don't want to learn a piano; it's old fashioned," I replied. "And I want to wear makeup for school like the other girls do."

"No," said my dad, "and you can get that muck off your face; you're 14." To which my mum replied, "Oh, maybe you could wear a tiny bit."

Wow, this was new, they were trying to make an effort as we never spoke before about things I would like to do, it felt weird so I agreed to return home.

Things were quite strange for the next few days at home; everything was quiet, almost like everyone was too scared to say anything, and I even had my favourite crispy pancakes for tea once, but then it was time to return to school.

I had been gone for over a month, so I was dreading going back to school, knowing everything would just be the same as before, I would continue to be bullied for the colour of my skin, and have people wanting to fight me, and have no friends, I didn't know what had happened these past few weeks at school, but I knew I would have work to catch up on.

Monday morning came, I got ready for school, and I even put a little bit of eye-liner on, much to my mom's disgust. As I walked into school and there was a queue outside the classroom, as usual, waiting for the teacher to unlock the door, something felt different. It felt like people were staring at me in the corridors. As I was standing at the back of the queue as always, I felt someone come behind me, grab me around the waist and pick me up and fling me around. Craig Nail was one of the popular boys and the boy who everybody in the class and year fancied. "Where have you been?" he said.

"What?" I replied.

"Everyone was worried about you."

I just stared at him, 'what' the hottest boy in the class, was concerned about me? And he was smiling at me? There was no name-calling, no anger or no hatred in his eyes. Was I dreaming?

"Who's this new girl?" I heard some people interrupt this very unusual moment between Craig and me.

They were teasing me because I had eye-liner on, but the tone had changed, their words weren't being followed up by Paki, or with anger in their voices, everyone was surrounding me. I didn't understand what was happening. The whole school knew about me, not just the people in my year, but people in the above and below years too. Everyone was trying to speak to me, and even more weirdly, Craig, who is the most popular boy in our year seemed to actually like me.

This mild popularity didn't last long; at all, the novelty of me being 'the missing girl' that everyone was talking about soon blew over, and regular service had resumed, the name-calling, the bullying all started again. Only this time, it hurt a lot more because I had now experienced a little bit of freedom, a little bit of time where I wasn't being bullied. I was out there in the big wide world, so to have to return to this bullying again hurt a lot. It was almost worse as the popular girls took a step down from their popularity for those few days when I was getting all the attention and that I was on top, and so now they had to make sure I was put back in my place, where they thought I belonged, beneath them.

However, a few girls tried to be my friend, Sharon Pens and Sonia Radcliffe, both of them on separate occasions stopped me in the corridor, asking about how I ran away, as they wanted to do this too. This was brilliant, I thought as I already know that buying sweets and doing homework for people didn't work these days to obtain friends, but now I held the key to doing something they wanted to do but didn't know how to. So, I could help them escape their lives too.

"Can you help me run away," Sonia asked.

"It's easy," I said, but seeing the opportunity to have a friend, I agreed. "Yes, I'll help you."

I told her to pack a bag and meet me outside her house at 2 o'clock in the morning. Things had kind of got back to normal at home too. Those few days of Mom and dad being lovely and having crispy pancakes were soon over, so I needed to get away again too, this might be easier this time, and I had someone to do it with. So once again in the early hours of the morning, I snuck downstairs and out the door, and went and met Sonia; however, this time there was no money, there was no Paul to come and rescue me, we had nowhere to go and no way of getting anywhere, so we just walked over the shops, and walked around the streets, Needless to say, we were soon spotted and took back home, and that was the end of that friendship.

Sharon Pens asked me to help her leave home, but she bottled it as soon as I was outside her house. But once again, I left the house in the early hours of the morning and couldn't go back. Still, all I could see was the chance of having a friend, and I knew that I couldn't stay at home when my parents had returned to their usual strictness and beatings, so this time when Sharon Pens didn't turn up, I didn't know what to do. So, I just spent the morning, which was now about 7:o'clock knocking on girls houses that I knew from school. Sonya Pierce was one of them; I knocked on the door, I asked if she was able to come out and play, and her mom came to the door with her and said "it's early in the morning; what are you doing out?"

"Nothing," I replied.

And once again, as I was only a few streets away from home, I was soon taken back.

This was the time of the school teacher strikes, meaning if a teacher was off sick or not in class for whatever reason, we would get sent home. Home was the last place I wanted to spend more time.

Craig and I were now secret friends, meaning if we saw each other outside of school, over the shops, or the park, we would chat and spend a bit of time together. Or we would have secret conversations in the school's corridors if no one saw. When he was with the rest of his friends, he wouldn't talk to me; he would then revert to being the popular boy. We were in a few classes together, and this one class was being sent home as there was no teacher available. So, as I walked through the gates to go home, Craig caught me up and asked where I was going.

"I don't know," I said, "but I don't want to go home."

Craig replied, "Well, there's no one in my house; you can come around mine if you want to."

It was a Thursday, and on a Thursdays, my mum would visit her friend in Ashmore Ave on the afternoons; her house was precisely opposite Craig's house, so if I went there, they would see me, and I would be in trouble again.

"Come in the back way," said Craig, as there was an alleyway at the side of his house, "and we will keep an eye on the time, so we can make sure we get you home at a time that you would usually be home for."

"OK," I agreed.'

Both Craig's parents were at work, so the house was empty, and I went along hoping no one would see me and Craig walking up the street together, because, after the whole Keith Jones experience, I didn't want girls wanting to fight me for having the audacity of talking to their Craig. Craig and I sat in his lounge at his house, just chatting about various things. I can't remember the exact subjects, but we were rattling away like friends do, and then out of the blue, and in the middle of my sentence, Craig said, "can I shag you?"

I was dumbstruck.

"Pardon?" I said, not truly believing what I heard.

"Can I shag you?" he said with an absolutely straight and serious face. And at that moment, I don't know what else I was thinking, but this was the first time I'd been with a boy on my own.

"Yes," I said instinctively.

It was that afternoon on Craig Nail's mother's lounge floor I lost my virginity and unbeknown to me, until years later, Craig told me it was when he lost his virginity too. The time had come when I had to run home, to arrive on time as though I had been to school all day. Craig was all of flummoxed as he gave me his shoes to put on instead of mine, but nothing was really said between us, except, "I've got to go," and that was it, I went home and never told anyone or stopped on the way.

My head was all of a blur with the antics of the afternoon. I had actually just lost my virginity, so that's what all the fuss is about, I thought, I can't say I enjoyed it, but what I did know was it really hurt. But now all I could think about was I felt like everyone hated me, I was constantly being bullied at school, I had no friends, and yet, I had just lost my virginity to the most popular boy in our year, the most good-looking boy in our year, the boy that everybody wanted to go out with. Nothing made sense in my head.

School mornings were like clockwork in our house. I would be called to get up, washed, have my breakfast, and out the door, and was never, late for school, never. Until the day after Craig and I slept together, for some reason, I was late for school, and it was one of those moments that you walked into class. Everyone turns around and looks at you; I was the last one into the class that morning. Everybody stared at me as I sped through the door and sat down as fast as I could; Craig just looked at me from the back of the class with half a smile; I felt like the whole class knew what had happened the day before, my stomach felt like it was on the floor, this was going to be something else they were going to bully me about, had he told everyone? Well, you only had to say to a couple of people in school, and then the whole school would know.

But he hadn't, he hadn't told anyone, of course, he didn't, the most popular boy in the year couldn't tell people that we had slept together, because then he would get bullied for sleeping with the Paki, for sleeping with that girl no one liked. So, it was business as usual, everything was the same as before, I kind of hoped that us sleeping together would then bring me into the popular gang, that he was in. But, still, it didn't; no one else knew about us. Everything just carried on as usual.

The time had come when we had careers officers in the school trying to find out what we wanted to do when we left school. I didn't really know; it was hard enough getting through school days without even thinking beyond school. So, when I was asked, what I wanted to be when I left school, I had no idea.

This was the time when Samantha Fox rose to fame along with Linda Lusardi and Maria Whittaker - Page 3 girls were everywhere you looked. There was always one of these girls on Page 3 in the national tabloid newspaper topless, and also in all the newspapers, some with their tops on some without. Everyone was talking about them, everybody liked them, and everyone was talking about them in a positive way, not a negative one. This reminded me of the girl I met when I ran away, Rachel, who was a kissogram girl, everybody loved her for those 15 minutes, she was in that pub, everybody loved her, and that's what I wanted, I wanted everyone to love me. So that's it! That's what I wanted to do, I wanted to be a model, and I'm even happy to be a page three girl remembering Rachel. Samantha Fox was only 16 when she did her first Page 3 shoot, and I wasn't far off that now. So, I told my mom and my careers officer. I wanted to be a model.

Mom took some pictures of me in a white basque and stockings just like Rachel had worn, in my bedroom just standing in front of my Billy Idol posters on the wall, I had no makeup on, just me in my underwear. She took the pictures of me with a disposable camera, and we had them developed. I went to the library and managed to find some names and addresses of model agencies in Birmingham and we sent the pictures off.

Word soon got out at school that I wanted to be a model. This gave everyone another reason to torment me; people would stand around me in the corridors making camera noises laughing at me,

"How can you be a model? You are a Paki, you're ugly, who's going to want to look at you?" they would jeer.

That's another thing that I was being bullied for, taunted and teased of the very thought that I could be a model. This was all too much now. I couldn't seem to do anything that's wasn't going to cause me to be bullied or teased or have friends. So, I had to try and remove some of the reasons I was being bullied. I would leave home with my oversized Duffle coat on, I would pretend I was hot, and I would take the coat off once I reached the corner of my road, and carry it to school; I would rather be freezing cold than for people to bully me because of my coat. I started not answering questions in class because I didn't want people taunting me for being a know-it-all. I hated every minute of being at school. I didn't mind the school work but I hated being at school, I was always a target. So, I started going into school to get my register mark. Then I would leave and just walk the streets on my own, or sit over the park, even in the rain, anything was better than being in school. I didn't need to actually stay at school much longer because I was determined I was going to be a model; I wanted that free feeling that I had those few weeks I ran away from home, not judged. I wanted to be adored, even if it meant getting my boobs out on a camera. I wanted that feeling that Rachel had in that pub.

Then I heard back from the agency.

CHAPTER TEN

Model Behaviour

"This came for you," said my mom, whilst handing me a simple, plain envelope.

What? I thought, I didn't have post, as I looked at the envelope, I noticed it had already been opened. If she wasn't telling me what's already inside, then I must be in trouble. I was still banned from seeing Jane, so I knew it couldn't be another telephone bill from the chat lines like before.

'Pauline Davidson agency would like to see you at her office, please call the following number to make an appointment.' the letter read.

I just looked at my mom, not entirely understanding what it meant. I didn't know whether to be excited or scared.

"It says they want to see me," I said nervously, knowing that there was no way I would be allowed to go to Birmingham.

"I know," said my mom; of course, she did, she'd already read the letter.

"I'll take you," she said.

"Really?" I replied, surprised.

"Yes, you don't think you're going on your own, do you?"

I didn't know whether to be happy, was this a good sign? Not only did one of the biggest modelling agencies in the country want to see me, but my mom was allowing me to go, and she was going to take me. But what if we went all the way to Birmingham only to be told that I'm too ugly, I'm not good enough, or my skin is too brown. My mom would be so angry; maybe I should say I don't want to go.

However, there was a tiny, tiny part of me that thought, surely, they wouldn't want to see me, just to tell me I was too ugly; they had the photographs of me, so they kind of knew what I looked like. But the photographs were not the same as seeing someone in person with brown skin. Instead, maybe, they see all the girls who send pictures to them, only to crush their dreams or change their mind when they arrive in their office. So, I really didn't know what to think or how to feel.

A few weeks later, the day had arrived, my mom and I took the bus to Birmingham, a journey I already knew, having taken it the year before as a runaway child trying to escape her horrendous life. Only this time, I was sitting comfortably with my mother by my side, going to see a woman who was either going to tell me what I already knew and was constantly being told throughout my life, which was I'm too ugly to be a model, and you're just a Paki. Or I would be shocked and told that, yes, people would pay to take pictures of you. However, the chance of that happening was excruciatingly minimal.

"Now, don't get showing me up," my mom said.

"I won't, "I replied.

"Just sit there, and don't speak until you're spoken to," she continued.

I just sat on the bus quietly, but inside my mind, I was psyching myself up for a whole world of the abuse I was already used to, except this would be coming from a woman who I didn't know, confirming everything I knew already. It was too late to turn around and go back home. The disappointment and hurt that I expected would be more bearable than my mom's anger for wasting her time.

As we arrived in Birmingham, my mom said, "I don't know where this place is, so we'll have to get a taxi."

I had never been in a taxi before; this was new. We walked towards a row of black cabs, I had only ever seen these on the TV so I was excited. As my mum and I sat in the back of this enormous cab, I couldn't help but tell her I felt like the queen as I waved my hand in a queenlike fashion out the window. My mom actually found this funny. Were we actually bonding over this experience? Of course, but I couldn't let myself get carried away because I knew everything was very shortly about to change.

Upon arrival at the agency, we both climbed out of the cab. We entered the building, 'Pauline Davidson Modelling Agency' read the shiny sign outside the door. My heart was pounding so hard, I don't belong here, this is going to be full of beautiful people, but we had gone that far, and there is no way I could of back out now. We walked into reception; it was bright, airy and light, the walls were covered in photographs of the most beautiful people I had ever seen, mainly girls, but I also noticed a few handsome men.

As I hid behind my mom, trying not to be seen in fear of being laughed at, the receptionist said sternly, "take a seat; I will let her know you're here."

I had never felt more insignificant or ugly in my whole life. I wished the chair would just swallow me up; I felt embarrassed, ashamed and really, really scared, let's just get this over with, just get through it. That's all I kept saying to myself in my head.

"Miss Vickers," the receptionist asked.

"Yes," said my mom, looking quite pleased with herself for being called Miss Vickers.

We both walked into the office, I could be quite clumsy so all I could think during this short walk to the lady's office was 'please don't fall over.'

"Take a seat," said the lady, who we assumed must be Pauline Davidson, as we sat down in a big office at the desk of a beautiful lady, she must have been in the early 40s, she had big curly, dark, 80s hair. "Thank you for sending your photographs in," she said.

I was sitting firmly in the chair next to my mom, trying not to have eye contact and definitely not wanting to speak.

"Well, this is something that she wants to do. I told her not to be stupid, no one's going to want you, but you know what kids are like when they have something in their head," said my mom.

The lady and my mom giggled. I just sat there feeling embarrassed. "I bet you get loads of kids wanting to be models and sending you photographs," said my mom trying to be amusing.

"Yes, I do," said Pauline Davidson, "we get about 2000 people sending me their photographs a week."

Wait, 2000 girls sent her their photographs with the same dream I had. How could I compete with that? There were only a couple of 100 other girls at my school, and every one of them was more attractive than I was, even the ugly ones. Now in this adult world, in a model agency where she receives 2000 requests a week, my heart just sank. Can we just go, please? Can we just get out of here? I was thinking. "But Susan" Pauline said.

Here it comes, here it comes, I thought.

"Stood out, above everyone else this whole month."

Yeah, I bet I did, what other brown skin girl would dare send their photographs in, I thought.

"She is stunning," Pauline continued.

What does that mean? I thought I'd never heard that word before. I just stared at her like I was the thickest person in the world.

"She has that something that none of my other girls have,

Yeah, brown skin, I thought, and I'm a Paki. I have never been so nicely and politely insulted before.

"You really have something, Susan" she said.

Yes, I know, stop dragging it out, please can we just leave? I thought. "Wait," said my mom. "So, are you telling me you chose her out of over 2000 other girls?" my mom asked.

"Yes," replied Pauline.

"So, you think she really could be a model?" my mum questioned. "Absolutely," Pauline replied.

"And I would love to have her on my books."

What?? My eyes must have popped out of my head on springs like the cartoons. I just stared at Pauline, frowning and really, really confused. Pauline just looked at me with a massive smile on her face, and I just looked at my mom, who too was smiling at me, something that didn't happen very often.

"You liked me?" I said, sounding about 5 years old.

"Yes," Pauline replied with a slight titter, "and not only that, I have international clients who are going to love you; you have that look which means you could carry off looking Spanish, Italian, or Portuguese and very few girls can do that."

My head was full of popping candy it seemed. However, I noticed she didn't use the word Paki or anything similar. Of course, she didn't, no one thanks Pakis are attractive, and then came the biggest question of all.

"Where are you from?" she queried.

Nooooooooo! I screamed in my head whilst mentally getting my coat. "People call me a Paki", I said,

"Oh!" Pauline replied. Her face had changed.

"Well, maybe don't tell people that, if I have an Italian client wanting to use you, then you are from Italy; if I have a Spanish client, then you're Spanish, but definitely don't tell them you're a Paki."

I am not a Paki, though, I said mentally but didn't have the nerve to say it out loud to her.

I couldn't believe my ears. I had never met anyone from abroad before.
"Do you have any other photographs?" Pauline asked.

"No," I said.

"Well, we need to get you a composite card made, as this is what I send to clients for them to choose the model they need.

A composite card was an 8 by 10-inch card, full of images of the model in different poses and styles. It also contained all your information like name, height and sizes, even your shoe size.

"I don't have one of those," I said.

They looked expensive, and we had no money, I thought my dream was in touching distance, and now it was being shattered again. So, I'll get a paper round, I thought, and earn some money to buy one.
"How old are you?" Pauline asked.

"14," replied my mom.

"Oh," there was that disappointing look on Pauline's face again.
"You are very young, so there may be a lot of work you won't be able to do just yet, but that will give you time to grow your hair a little longer."

I still had the boy cut my mom gave me.

"Most photographers will give you copies of the photos they take, so we can build a portfolio for you", said Pauline optimistically.
This was like a vast book, almost like a big photo album. It was to showcase all the different looks you have for photographers to see the different styles you can do.

"So, people are actually going to pay me to take my picture?" I asked.
"Yes," Pauline replied, giggling again.

"You will be great," she said.

None of this made sense in my head. Just because I wanted to be a model didn't mean I could actually be a one. After all these years of having been bullied and taunted and abused because of how I looked and such negativity around my skin colour, it was so surreal to hear someone say it's because of how I looked that people will love me. My head was like an explosion.

"So we will be in touch," Pauline said, reaching out a hand to shake my mom's hand and then mine.

"Welcome to the agency Susan," she said as she took my hand.
"Thank you," I replied.

And we left. How I didn't just wet myself all over the floor or be sick, I have no idea, and then we left the agency for the journey home. The journey back to Wolverhampton felt different.

"I'm going to be a model," I said to my mom.

"Yes, you are," she replied.

After that, everything felt warmer, with my mom, more bonded and just lovely. We got off the bus at the precinct by our house as mom needed to go to the shop. As usual, mom would spend a few minutes in each shop chatting to the people who work there. Only this time I could hear her saying "My daughter is going to be a model."

The shopkeeper replied, "Who? Susan?" they questioned.

Of course, it had to be me; I was the only one that had to go to the shops with my mom. Her other daughter Carole never did.

"Yes," my mom replied with a smile on her face.

But, hold on, this was new. Did my mum actually say something positive about me? And did she actually seem a little bit proud? And almost bragging? This whole day was a mind fuck.

We got home, and we told my dad.

"So that means she can start bringing money into the house and paying her way," my mom said to my dad.

And there it was, there was me being overwhelmed that my mom might have actually been proud of me, or happy for me, but really all she thought about was that I would be earning some money, which of course I had to give to her just like my dad did every week.

And so, my modelling career began. I would attend deportment classes and visit various photographers who took many photographs of me for my composite card. The pictures were primarily black and white, and I loved them. I couldn't believe it was me, but most of all, I loved the fact that you couldn't really tell that my skin was brown. And then my first big modelling job came in. It was for an airline company that made trips to the Far East. So, I had to look like a Geisha girl, in full kimono, my air up in a bun, and I had to be at the agency at 1:00 PM on Saturday.

By this time, I had already started to earn some money, so I hired a kimono from a fancy dress shop and purchased the makeup to do my face. McDonald's had an offer on Chinese week; this meant they were giving away free chopsticks with every burger.

Saturday came, and I put on my kimono and the slippers that came with it, managed to get my hair in a bun on top of my head as it was now much longer and put chopsticks into my bun. Then came the makeup; as we know, Geisha girls have a particular look, so I had to paint my face white! Oh, the irony, I wanted to have white skin all my life, but this was extreme. I actually looked great. So, off I went, completely forgetting that I now had to get a bus into town, walk across town, to the train station, get the train to Birmingham, walk across Birmingham City centre, to another train station, and catch the train to Sutton where the agency was. All this dressed as a Geisha girl. This had to be one of the most bonkers times of my teenage years. Of course, I was used to people staring at me, so I wasn't too bothered, although I did have a few people, usually old ladies coming up to me saying, "You look lovely," I have never had that before, a complete stranger approaching me to tell me I look lovely. But of course, I did. I looked nothing like me.

I knocked on the agency door; Pauline opened the door with a massive smile on her face and said, "You look fabulous, come in."

So that embarrassing journey was worth it. However, when I walked into the agency and saw all the other girls on the same job, No one had a kimono on or the makeup.

"Have I got the wrong day?" I asked Pauline.

"No," she said; these girls are going to get ready now.

What? Wait, I thought.

"So, I didn't have to make that whole two-hour journey dressed like this? I could have just got ready here like everyone else?" I questioned Pauline.

"That's what you should do, Susan; you get ready when you get to the job, so everything is fresh," she replied.

Well, I never felt so embarrassed, but Pauline thought it was hilarious, which put me at ease, so I just sat in the studio and waited patiently for all the other girls to get ready and then off we went to Sutton Park for the photoshoot. And it was great until I realised I had to make that excruciating bus and train journey back home to Wolverhampton, still dressed like a Geisha girl.

I started to meet many other girls in the deportment classes and the model shoots, and again, it was just like school, I was always the only brown person there. There was one black girl I saw a couple of times, but I was the only person with brown skin. Sometimes when there were shoots with a few other girls, I would see a few of them jostling so as not be the person that stood next to me in the photographs.

I would hear them saying, "No, you go there," one would say. "I don't go to go there, you go there," said another, as they pushed each other to be the person standing next to me.

They thought I didn't hear them. A couple of times, some of the photographers would take 10s of photographs of some of the girls, but only a couple of me and sometimes none at all. My agent used to say, not to worry; mine wasn't the look they looked for at that time. They are always looking for a particular look when they book models. But in my head, I knew even though I was now a model, some people still didn't like the look of me or what being brown represented.

So, I had to think about looking like I was from any European country than my actual race. I started to change the way I dressed. I was now 16. I had a place of my own and began to dress as differently as possible, so people and photographers would not think I was a Paki.

Susan's very first modelling shoot and composite card aged 14. Bottom left Newspaper cutting from Susan's very first model agency and photography studio .

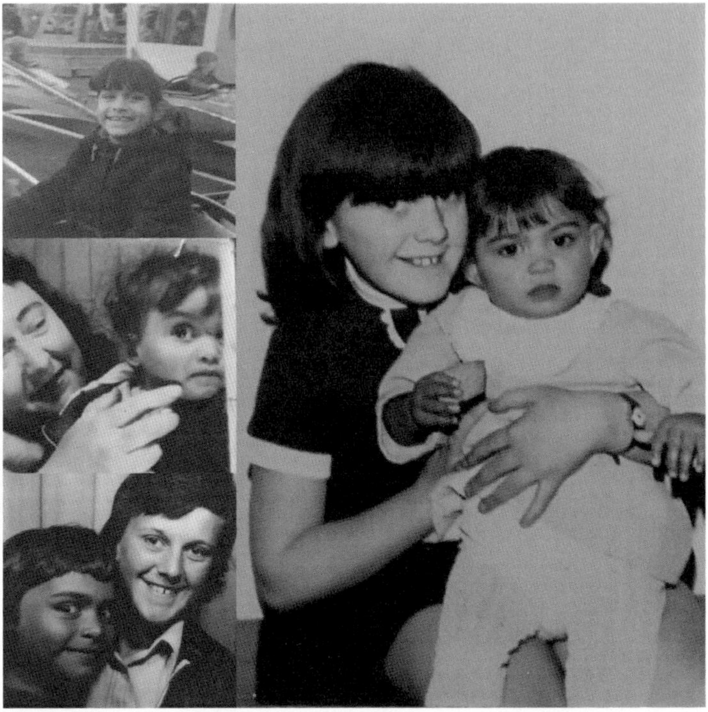

Top left Susan enjoying the fun fair aged circa 8 years old.
Middle left Freda and Susan circa 12 months old.
Bottom left Susan aged 7 with sister Carole aged circa 16.
Right main picture Carole aged 11 with sister Susan 18 months old.

Main picture wedding of Pamela and Tony
Top right young Ray and Freda , and 60 years married.
Middle right, Freda and Ray on honeymoon in Blackpool 1960.
Bottom right, family members of Pamela who were ok with the wedding .

Current photographs of Susan still modelling today.

I was seven stone and really skinny, so I would wear skirts the size of a postage stamp, heels as high as skyscrapers and I had a big, colossal mop of 80s curly hair. I didn't wear much makeup only because I was no good at putting it on without it making me look like a doll, but occasionally, I liked to put a little bit of lipstick on. I now had my first proper boyfriend, it was a wonderful change to actually have someone who found me attractive and wanted to be with me, He was a bit of a ladies' man, and all the girls fancied him, and he fancied all the girls. He had a car as he was a couple years older than me. We didn't do much together as I was still very young. We would drive around in his car and go up the Beacon which was an abandoned air-raid shelter not far from where we lived. We used to sit there and eat roe and chips almost every night, well until my skin started to turn yellow from the batter dye, which was highly amusing. Some nights, usually a weekend he would go to a club. He wouldn't take me with him, as I was too young.

One night I thought I would surprise him, as I looked much older than my age, so it was no problem for me to get into the club. As soon as Wayne saw me, he tried to hide, so I started asking a couple of the girls if they'd seen Wayne.

"Why do you want to know?" they asked.

"I'm his girlfriend," I would reply.

"No, you're not," they laughed.

"Yes, I am," I would argue.

However, word soon spread around the club that someone calling themselves Wayne's girlfriend was looking for him. Eventually, Wayne grabbed my arm and led me outside, asking what I was doing there as I was embarrassing him.

"I thought I would surprise you," I said.

"Go home," he replied. Everyone's taking the piss, telling me I'm with a Paki," he was so angry. And with that, I left.

A few days later, Wayne apologised, and we made up; I think he was more embarrassed because he used to tell girls he was single. To prove he was serious about me, he took me to meet his parents. They had a big house in Coseley, Wolverhampton. We pulled up, and we walked inside. His family were German, and he introduced me to his mother, "This is Susan, my girlfriend," he said to the lady who looked like a prison officer.

I wasn't even sure if it was a lady as she had such a deep scary voice and wore men's trousers and looked very butch, she just stared at me. "Are you a Paki?" she said bluntly.

Shocked, I replied, "No."

"Come here, you," she said to Wayne as she walked out of the room, leaving me standing there on my own.

"What are you doing bringing one of them home?" I heard her ask Wayne.

"She's my girlfriend," Wayne said.

"Well, if you're going to be with one of them, you're no son of mine. You know what you can do," she shouted.

And with that, I heard a door slam. Wayne just said, "Let's go," and off we went.

"Why doesn't she like me?" I asked.

"Just ignore them," he said.

"She won't let me go back there now," he said.

"Well, don't tell her you're not seeing me anymore?"

But, of course, I was used to being a secret. But his parents promptly kicked him out, so we went to find a flat of our own.

My life during my late teens was such a confusing time; the modelling now gave me the confidence I never had before, for the most part. I was being paid for people to actually take my photograph. I was travelling all over the world for photographic shoots and advertising shoots. When work was a little slow, I was also the resident model in a substantial photographic studio in Birmingham. They would hold photography nights where people from photography clubs and photographic magazines would come and take pictures of a few other girls and me in the different studios. Photographers often would turn up or ask for their money back from the studio or refuse to take pictures of me because they just didn't find brown skin attractive. But then others loved that they had never photographed anyone with brown skin before.

Outside of the studio, I was still getting regular abuse in the streets, name-calling, people I worked with, strangers I would see out. Social media wasn't around in those days. Still, basically, people shouting abuse out of car windows or anonymously across a bar or in the shopping centers would be the equivalent of trolling these days. The extremes in my life were vast. One minute I would be in front of a camera being told I was beautiful, and the next minute, I was having racist abuse thrown at me left, right and center. People in restaurants would ask to move tables or request that the managers not sit me next to them.

By the time I was 26, I had two photographic studios and a model agency of my own. I was one of the prominent judges for many beauty pageants, Miss Aston Villa, Miss Wolves, Miss West Midlands, even Mr UK. The irony was massive. Here I was spending my 26 years of life being judged, abused and tormented because of how I looked and yet here I was sitting on a panel as a judge, judging other people in front of me on their looks. I had many people not wanting to shake my hand or do business with me because they didn't want to be seen to be associated with a Paki, but I am not a Paki, I would plead, some people would refuse to even shake my hand.

My photograph was always in the local newspaper for various things, my business was thriving, but none of this prevented me from having to constantly chant, "I am not a Paki, I am not a Paki."

I had a new boyfriend who was a fellow model. He was the spitting image of Jude Law; we were so in love, but he had a temper, and whenever we argued, he would hold me down on the sofa in a rage, screaming in my face.

"You are going to die a very lonely old woman; you are just a Paki, no one else would want you; you should be grateful I'm with you. Who wants to be with a Paki?" he would scream.

I had no defence to this abuse, except the usual 'I am not a Paki' I couldn't help the way I looked. Not much seemed to have changed from school except the venue, racist comments, abuse, name-calling, the spitting in my face, and the disgust some people had because of my skin colour was insurmountable, as the bullies in school. But now, I was an adult, and the people abusing me were adults. This hurt much more now, because as an adult, I now understood the hatred behind the name-calling, I could feel the anger and disgust towards me, and this was all coming from adults who were very aware of what they were saying, not children who had no fundamental understanding of the pain it caused every time. I would get into an argument with a boyfriend, or if I accidentally knocked someone in the club, instantly, I would be taunted with hurtful, hateful, horrible name-calling. How can the people I love and care for be so awful and cruel towards me? Nothing made sense.

Was this constant abuse ever going to stop? I don't think so. Will I ever stop trying to convince people that I'm not a Paki? Maybe these racists could see something in me that I was unaware of? Perhaps I really was a Paki? But my mum told me I wasn't. I've been denying it my whole life, but what if it was true? No, it can't be.

I needed to find out once and for all.

CHAPTER ELEVEN

Certified

My mom had previously told me that my real mother was white, blonde and blue-eyed, which meant that my 'foreignness' must be mainly off my father.

"What did my dad look like?" I asked my mom.

"I can't remember," said my mom, "we only saw him briefly in the courts when you were adopted."

"So, what did he look like then?" I asked again.

"He just had dark hair and tanned skin," she replied.

"But, where was he from? Was he a Paki?"

"How do I know?" my mother replied.

"Well, did he look like one?" I continued.

"I don't know, Susan," mother snapped back, seemingly annoyed at all the questions.

"Well, you are old enough now," interrupted my dad, "why don't you have a look for them?"

"Why would I look for someone who didn't want me?"

I have enough of that in my day-to-day life now, I thought.

"Well, we're not your real mom and dad," my mom said.

"But you are my mum and dad; I don't want to meet them. Why would I? What for?" I said.

I had never thought for one second about meeting my real family; it just sounded like torture; why would I meet someone so heartless to give away a tiny, innocent baby? I already didn't like them; what could they possibly say to me which would make this feeling better?

I had never thought that I would ever see them, let alone want to meet them. So why would I want to meet a man whose skin colour meant I had so much pain and heartache in my life. But hold on, maybe I didn't have to meet them, perhaps I could just find out where they are and see what they look like. At least that would give me some idea; plus, as I was at the peak of my modelling career, I didn't have very big boobs, so I would also see from looking at my real mother if my boobs were going to grow any bigger.

"But, remember you can't just go interrupting other people's lives," my dad piped up.

"What?" I replied.

"Well, they have their own lives too now, and families of their own, so they might not want you disrupting that, "dad continued.

I couldn't believe what I was hearing, "What!" I replied, "They didn't care about my feelings when they gave me away, so why should I care about theirs?"

"You can't just do that," said my dad, "They may not have told their new families about you."

"I really don't give a shit if I disrupt their lives," I said, "They didn't care about my feelings when they gave me away."

I was now angry with my dad; how did he care more about their feelings than mine? It didn't make sense to me. Besides, I didn't even want to meet them. I said I just wanted to see what they look like.

"Where did they live?" I asked.

"I don't know," said my mom, "we weren't allowed to know that information."

"What were their names?" I asked.

My mum was looking agitated at me asking these questions.

"Susan, I can't remember, it was a long time ago, all I remember was she looked like a slapper, I think her name was Pat, Pamela or something like that."

And there she was again, my mom saying cruel things about people, well, not just any people, only people indirectly connected to me, of course.

"What do you mean?" I asked.

"Well, she used to walk around dressed like a prostitute," said my mom.

"There's no need for that," my dad jumped in.

"Well, she did," snapped back my mom.

I wasn't too bothered about what she said about my real mother because I didn't like them anyway, and my mom being slightly on the heavy side, was always jealous of anyone slimmer than her.

"All we've got is your birth certificate," she said.

"Can I have a look? Does it say anything on there?" I asked.

"I don't know where it is; it's upstairs somewhere," mom replied.

"Well, can I get it?" I asked.

"You're not going messing in my bedroom," she said, "and I'm certainly not going to go looking for it now," she continued.

"When then?" I asked.

Mom was getting angry, "I will do it when I'm ready, not when you want me to," she snapped.

And with that, I'd hit a brick wall again. I was no further on with my understanding of who I was.

A few weeks later, when visiting my mum and dad, I asked to use the toilet. I didn't really want the loo; I just wanted the opportunity to sneak into their bedroom to look for my birth certificate. There was an old First aid box in one of their drawers with lots of paperwork in. but the floorboards in my parents' bedroom were really creaky, and the medical box was made of tin, so I had to be really careful in what movements I made. I also knew I couldn't take too long. I scrambled through the box as fast as I could, hoping the right piece of paper would just pop up in front of me.

I found a small square piece of paper which was red and white. Certificates of birth, it said at the top. Found it! Susan Paula Vickers born 26th of January 1970, father Raymond Fredrick Charles Vickers, and that's it, nothing else. It had no other information except that of mom and dad and me! I folded it back up put it back in the box; there had to be something else, I continued to search. Still, time was ticking on, so frustrated I put it back in the middle of the pile of documents, closed the tin and went downstairs, flushing the toilet as I went to continue the lie that I had gone to the toilet.

Bloody hell, what could I do now? I was none the wiser. I had no names of my original parents. I didn't know where they lived or anything at all really. So, I certainly didn't know where to start looking.

I was still a member of the local library, which in those days was the primary source of anything you needed to know and the equivalent of the Internet today. So off I went.

"How can I find out who my real parents are?" I asked the librarian.
"What do you mean?" she replied.

"Well, I'm adopted."

"All the books about giving birth are over there," she said as she pointed to a row of books.

"OK," I said, as I walked over to the shelf picking up various books, all these books were about motherhood and giving birth. These were no good. I went back to reception.

"There's nothing there," I said to the same lady.
"Have you looked at all of them?" she asked.

"Yes," I replied.

"What do you want to actually know?" she asked.

I explained, I wanted to find my real parents, and I didn't know where to go.

"Oh," she said, "well, why don't you phone the council?"

"Why would I call the council? They give people houses," I asked.

"They do more than that," she replied.

"Social services, they might be able to help you," and she gave me a telephone number to call, "or you could just go up the Civic Centre", she said.

I left feeling frustrated and no further on, but I was on a mission once I had something in my head. The council wasn't going to be able to help, I thought, but I also had nothing to lose, and so I headed off up to town.

I need to speak to someone who knows where my parents are?" I said to the lady in the reception of the Civic Centre.

"Pardon?" she replied.

So, I very quickly told her my plight.

"You will need to speak to someone in social services," she said.

"Oh no, not them again," I thought, as my previous experience with social services from when I ran away, as they just talked me into going back home when I didn't really want to.

"What's your name?" asked the receptionist. "I will get someone to come down and see you."

"Susan Vickers," I said.

"And what's your date of birth?"

I told her and then sat down and waited patiently.

"Susan Vickers?" I heard my name called, "Would you like to come this way?" said a lady.

I was going to have 1001 questions, or I was going to be told I was not allowed to look for my real parents, I thought, but I followed her into a room.

"How can I help?" she asked.

"I want to find my real mom and dad," I said.

"Why?" she asked.

"I just want to know where I come from, that's all."

"What did your mum and dad tell you?" she asked.

"They don't know anything," I said.

"Well, there are rules," she said, "We can't just tell you where to find your birth parents."

Birth parents, so that's what they're called.

The lady continued "People who are born before November 1975 have to go through social services to be able to obtain their birth records if they were adopted."

"What does that mean?" I asked.

"You have to have an appointment with a social worker who will go through the process with you; it's not a quick and easy process; there are procedures," she said.

"OK," I said.

"Shall I make you an appointment to see someone?"

"Yes, please," I replied.

"You will need to bring a form of ID and your birth certificate with you," she said.

"OK," I said.

And of I went with an appointment card in my hand to return in a couple of weeks.

Now I had to convince my mum to give me my birth certificate.

A few days later, I went to my mum and dad's house and told them I'd been up to the Civic Centre.

"I have an appointment to go back, but they've told me I need to take my birth certificate," I said while showing my appointment card to my mom.

"You are a pain in the arse," said my mom.

"But I need it", I pleaded.

"You'll have to come back tomorrow; I'm not looking for it now," she said.

And so, I did.

A few weeks later, I found myself back at the Civic Centre with my medical certificate, birth certificate and National Insurance card in my hand to prove who I was.

"Come through," I heard a voice say.

She was a little old lady; she looked pretty similar to Mrs. Cattermole, the headmistress at my primary school. So, we sat down in a plain, cold room with nothing but a desk and a couple of chairs.

"I understand you want to find your birth parents," she said.

"Yes, do you know where they are?" I enquired.

"Well, we do hold some records here, but you will have to get your original birth certificate before we can release them.

"OK, how do I do that?" I asked.

"Well, tell me a little bit more about yourself," she said, "and why you want to find them."

And it was with that I went on to explain to her about me being bullied and my parents not knowing anything and that everyone thought I'm a Paki.

"I'm constantly called a Paki, but my mum and dad said I'm not one, I don't know anything, I don't know who I am or what I am," I said. Luckily, I grew up in the same town as I still lived in, which was the same town I was adopted, and the same council that dealt with the adoption.

"We do hold the records here," continued a social worker, whose name I now knew to be Mary Woods, "but we're not allowed to give them to you unless you have your birth certificate."

"I have; I said it's here," as I gave her the small piece of paper.

She looked at it and said, "This isn't your birth certificate. This is just a copy of your adoption record, we need your original certificates of birth, which is a much bigger piece of paper, but you can only get them from Stafford, where they hold births and death records. We will contact them, and arrange for you to pick up your original birth certificate, which you will have to pay for."

"OK," I said.

"Are you sure this is what you want?" asked Mary.

"Yes," I replied; I was happy to do whatever it took to find out the truth of who I am.

"OK, we will send you a letter with an appointment to go and pick up your original document," said Mary.

And off I went.

CHAPTER TWELVE

"Which one are you?"

It was a dull dreary day as we headed off to Stafford, it felt like Doomsday. I had my Jude Law boyfriend with me, and despite him calling me a Paki many, many times in arguments, he wanted to find out what was in the envelope too, only for different reasons. He found the whole situation funny. I definitely did not, I needed his support and understanding, but how could he understand? I just had to deal with this turmoil myself as usual.

As we stood on the motorway bridge under the grey skies and the noisy traffic below, my heart felt as though it was actually breaking. For the last 21 years I had hoped for the 'happy ever after' but now I found myself glued to the envelope and I couldn't bring myself to open it. What if the contents of the envelope meant I had to continue to live the rest of my life the way it had been so far?

I moved a few steps away from my boyfriend, and I started to open the envelope really slowly, almost in the hope that it would disintegrate in my hands like some secret mission as a sign not to open it. I took out the piece of paper, which was a lot bigger than the birth certificate I had from my mom. As I unfolded it, my heart was beating so fast and loud I could almost hear it.

Please, please, please, I couldn't stop saying in my head. I slowly unfolded the top part of the paper.

'Susan Paula Kainth.

OK, so far, so good. That doesn't sound that foreign. So, I continued to unfold the rest of the paper.

Father: Jaswant Singh Kainth.

The whole world felt like it had stopped.

Noooooooooo, please, no, oh my God, oh my God, oh my God, this can't be happening. It's a mistake. Please kill me now. My throat went dry, and I felt like I had a bowling ball in the pit of my stomach.

As I read further along the columns it said:

Nationality: Indian

I'M DONE.

My legs buckled, which made me grab onto the railing so tightly to stop my fall, tears flooded uncontrollably down my face, inside I could not hear my heart beating at all now. All I could hear was this internal scream. My life was done, all my worst fears had come true, nothing, nothing could be worse than this. I tried to look at the paper again, but I could barely read it with the tears constantly filling my eyes.

My boyfriend peered at the paper and just burst out laughing; as he walked away from me, he thought this was the funniest thing ever and had no understanding at all. But, of course, he didn't; he was a white, blonde, blue-eyed model, his look was totally acceptable in the world.

I was just sobbing, I was sobbing so hard my tears ran out, I had none left, in my whole body. I tried looking at the document again, hoping it said something different, but it didn't. I continued to read.

Mother: Pamela Fellows.

Nationality: British.

Well, at least that was something. But, as I stared at my certificate, it seemed that the word' Indian' and 'Singh' were the only words I could see clearly; they seemed almost three dimensional, standing out on the whole of the page. Not only were my worst, most worst fears confirmed, but they were also made much more significant by the fact that my father probably wore a turban too. How could it possibly be much worse?

How had my life become much worse than it already was? People who called me names, I would actually be lying to deny them now, to deny who I was. How could I turn around when being called a Paki to defend myself by saying, "actually, I'm not a Paki; I am half Indian" how would that be any better? In their minds, I would still be a Paki. It was all the same to them.

As I walked back to my car, my boyfriend was still giggling at this revelation.

"It's not funny," I said.

"I still love you," he replied as he continued to laugh.

That didn't make me feel any better. What did that mean? I still love you even though you are Paki? It didn't make me feel any better at all.

My head was hurting, and my heart was broken; all these certificates confirmed was that the rest of my life would definitely be spent being continually being called a Paki, and there was nothing I could do about it, nothing, I'm going to have to lie for the rest of my life. If I lied hard enough, then people would have to believe me, if I did everything, absolutely everything that so-called Pakis don't do, they would have to believe I am not one, and then maybe, just maybe the name-calling and the abuse would stop. So, what I would do is lie and deny until my dying day. It's the only way I believed my life would be bearable.

Armed with my original birth certificate I made another appointment to go back and see the social worker. A few days later I was sitting back in the office in the council, and ready to be told anything they knew.

"Do you have any questions?" asked Mary Woods.

"Not really," I said.

But, of course, I didn't; I knew everything I needed to know and everything I didn't want to know.

"Would you like to meet your mom?" she asked.

"No," I replied "what for? She gave me away."

"Some people like to meet their birth parents, so they can ask any questions they would like to know the answers to."

"No," I said, "I've got nothing to say to her."

"You have no questions at all? Aren't you curious to find out what happened?" asked Mary.

"I know what happened, they didn't want me, so they gave me away," I said.

"Sometimes, it's not as simple as that," said Mary, "I have printed off the records that we have about your adoption," she pushed an envelope towards me, "have a think about it, take a look through these when you get home. You can always give me a call, and we can have another chat."

She continued, "If you do want to meet her, maybe we could you simply write her a letter, and tell her you have been in touch with us, and ask her if she would like to meet you. Would you be happy to do that?"

"You're not going to tell her about me?" I asked.

"No, we are not allowed to give any information about you or your whereabouts; we're only allowed to give the adoptee any information we know about their birth parents, and all that information is in that envelope," she said.

"Maybe she wouldn't want to see me; why would she? She gave me away?" I said.

"Sometimes, children are reunited with their birth parents, and everything is wonderful, like they have a new family," Mary said.
I didn't have a great relationship with my family, but what if my real family were kinder and nicer and loved me for me regardless of the colour of my skin.

"I don't know," I said.

"Well, go away, have some time to think about it, and call me when you are ready. I won't do anything unless you ask me to do so," Mary said.

What if my real family lived in a big house, had nice things, and welcomed me into loving normal family life? That would be like a dream.

"I don't know what to think," I said.

"That's OK," Mary replied "take some time and think about it, and call me if you change your mind if you want to write a letter, we can pass it on to her."

"No, I wouldn't know what to say. I have nothing to say. I don't know," I said, all confused.

"Have a think and call me anytime; we can always talk about it again," said Mary.

With that, I left.

As I opened the envelope that Mary gave me, inside was the report about my real parents, it didn't really tell me too much, except that my real mother's name was Pamela and of course, my father's name which I already knew. However, he also had an English name, Tony; the document said that Pamela had already got a son called Tilly born before me.

That meant I have a brother, I thought; what kind of name is Tilly? So, I continued to read. It said that Pam and Tony struggled financially and couldn't afford to keep me. My parents didn't have much, but they still managed I thought.

This made me dislike her even more, but I continued to read, 'after giving Susan up for adoption, Pamela became pregnant again and they had another baby girl, which they named Emma Michelle.'

What! Oh my God, I have a sister too, but hold on, did they now have money to have another child? I continued to read, 'Emma was also given up for adoption and went to a loving family in Wombourne.' What the hell! I thought, what is going on? I couldn't make any sense or reason in my head. So, she had another child after me and gave her up too? These people are evil, pure evil. I started to get really angry, so now I have a sister too who was also given up for adoption like me. Now I seem to have more questions in my head than ever.

Wait, that means there's someone else out there just like me. I have a sister with the same mom and dad, who is adopted too. I wonder what she's like? I wonder if she had the same treatment in life as I did? Oh, so many questions but not so many answers.

I spent the next few days just staring at the papers in front of me, and mainly at my birth certificate, breaking my own heart over and over and over again. Still, now my curiosities were pricked, and I needed to know more, so I made another appointment to see Mary Woods.

"How do you feel now?" asked Mary.

"I don't know," I replied, "do you know anything about my sister?"

"We are not allowed to tell you anything about siblings; we are only allowed to tell you about your birth parents," she said.

"You can't tell me anything about her at all? What she's like? Or what she looks like?"

"We can't tell you anything; all we can to tell you is what's in that document. If you want to try and find your sister yourself, you can; we cannot help you with that. How do you feel about meeting Pamela?" she asked.

“No, I do not want to meet her. They could have found a way to keep me, and not only that, she then gave up another child. So, she mustn’t be a nice person. Who has children and gives them away not once but twice?” I said.

“Sometimes there’s more to it than that, you could always ask her those questions, if they are important to you, maybe write her a letter asking what you want to know.”

“No,” I said.

“Maybe she could write you a letter and send it to us to give you?”

“What could she possibly say that could make all of this right?” I asked.

“Sometimes people have to make difficult choices, and we don’t always know the full circumstances, sometimes it’s tough for mothers or parents to give away their children, maybe if you met her, you might get some closure,” Mary said.

“No,” I replied. I was so stubborn.

“It might help, it might help you come to terms with everything you’ve been through.”

“How could it possibly help? How could it possibly make all these years of bullying and heartache better? “I asked.

“Maybe give her a chance to explain?” said Mary “, and if nothing comes of it, you never have to see her again.”

I don’t know, I thought; I already hated this woman for making me live the life that I have, but then what if she didn’t want to see me anyway? What if she didn't want to know? What if it was a mistake? Who makes those kinds of mistakes? Oh, I don't know, so much was going around in my head.

"She might not want to see me," I said to Mary.

"How about we write her a letter and ask her? We can tell her you've been in touch with us, and we can take it from there?" she said.

Why should I? I thought, why should she have any knowledge of me? How I'm doing? And what I look like? She didn't care back then, so why should I be bothered now? But then I thought why should she also get away with this? Then it came to me. I'm going to tell her, I'm going to say to her face, how awful my life has been because of her, because of what they did, I'm going to have a little go at her, this was all her fault, both of their faults.

"OK, well, maybe just let her know I have made an inquiry, and we will see what she says," I said.

"OK," said Mary ", I will write to her, and tell her you have been in touch and I will let you know what she says."

And with that, I left her office.

I have always been a curious person. I want to know the ins and outs of everything, the reasons why, how, when, what and, in all walks of my life, basically I'm just really nosy.

I couldn't stop thinking about Pamela and Tony. What could have been going through their heads? Conversations they had? But mostly what they looked like? Social services didn't hold any photographs of either of them, the only image I had in my head was what my mum told me of a blonde, blue-eyed lady who wore short skirts. People always say if you want to know what a girl will look like when they're older, then look at their mother. But of course, I didn't have that luxury. I had never met her, I still wasn't really that interested in meeting her, but the curiosity of seeing what they both looked like was so prominent in my mind. I just wanted to see what she looked like; that's all I could think of.

I took another look at my original birth certificate; it had an address there; Bilston was only a few miles away from where I lived and in the same town. But, oh my God, I could have literally walked past her at any time or even many times, not knowing who she was.

I went back to the library and asked to look through the electoral rolls. Fellows, Pamela Fellows, there were quite a few, as I continued my search, Bilston! That's the same address as what's on my birth certificate! I checked the dates on the electoral rolls, oh my God, oh my God, she still lives at the same address, and there were other people with the same last name living there too. So, the whole family still lived at the same address. This is ridiculous. I've got to go, and see what the house is like. I've got to go and see where my real mother lives.

I now had my first car, a Ford Capri mark one in white, by this time. I loved it. There wasn't much room inside, but I really loved it, so myself and my boyfriend jumped in the car and drove to Bilston.

I had all kinds of expectations in my head. For someone to still live in the same house for all of these years, it must be a big beautiful house, with lots of bedrooms, and hanging baskets and beautiful flowers in the garden, one of those big drives that you drive up and can park six cars on. A place where the streets are clean and everything is quiet. So, with an A-to-Z street map, we turned into their estate, where we could find her road.

"Oh," I said as I stared out the window at all the dull, boring, scruffy council houses, "It's not very nice around here," I said.

Maybe she lives in the posh part; every estate has a posh part I thought. So, we continued up the main road, saw the sign for her street, took the turn, and the houses still looked the same one by one my high expectations started to disappear.

"Pullover," I said to my boyfriend who was driving, "that's it, that's the one," I said, pointing to the house just in front of us.

It was nothing special, in the street full of council houses, this one was actually OK, it looked clean, it had flowers in the garden, but you could still tell it was a council house, just a tiny, tiny bit nicer than the rest of them in the street.

"Pull back a bit I said, so I could just sit staring at the house without anyone seeing.

We pulled up on the opposite side of the road and just sat staring at the house, trying to imagine what she was doing in there, what it looked like; we stayed there for a while; what if she came out of the house? I thought I would just duck, I still didn't want to meet her, but I did want to see what she looked like, the hours came and went, and there were no signs of movement, we called it a day and went back home.

We went back each afternoon for the next few days and just sat on the opposite side of the road watching her house.

"She might not live there anymore," said my boyfriend, "she might have moved."

"No, she can't have done," I replied.

"Shall I go and knock on the door and ask?" he said.

"No!" I snapped back, "I'm not ready; she might answer the door, she might see me, now let's just wait; she has to come out at some time."

But what if he was right? What if she didn't live there anymore and we were looking at some strangers' house.

"Drive up the street a little bit," I asked.

"Why?" he said.

"I'm going to try something," we pulled about five houses away from Pamela's home.

I got out of the car and knocked on a random house.

"What are you doing?" shouted my boyfriend.

"Shhhhhh" I said.

The door opened, and a young woman said hello.

"Hello," I said, "I have just driven down from Blackpool; I am Pamela Fellow's cousin, and I can't remember which house she was living at, do you know?"

I couldn't believe what I was saying. The woman looked at me strangely and said "Pamela Fellows? She looked confused, "does she have blonde hair?" she asked.

"Yes," I said, "that's the one."

"Oh," she replied ", it's that house there," as she pointed across the road. "That one?" I pointed too to confirm which house she meant.

"Yes, that's the one," she said confidently.

"OK, thank you so much," and I walked back up the path to the car as fast as I could.

"Drive, drive, quick," I said.

"Where to?" said my boyfriend.

"Just drive", I snapped.

As we pulled out of the street, I said "We have got the wrong house; it's the one opposite."

"What?" said my boyfriend "Oh my God."

Pamela lived in the house that we had been sitting right outside of, not the house opposite. As usual, my boyfriend found this so funny, whereas I was completely panicked, she could have seen me at any moment. She could have even been watching me, watching the house opposite. So, this is all a disaster. So, we went back home and returned the next day, only this time we positioned ourselves on the opposite side of the road in order to watch the correct house this time.

The house looked just like most of the others in the street, it was very plain, it was semi-detached, it didn't have any flowers in the garden, it's had thick net curtains, and it was a straightforward house, it was two houses away from a Cul de sac.

We went each afternoon and sit for hours watching the house for the next few days. One afternoon some boys were playing Kerby in the street right outside her home, one of the boys was black, and he was the spitting image of me, only darker, but he did have a beautiful smile. Oh my God, that could be my brother, I thought, as I knew from the paperwork, I had a brother called Tilly. As I continued to watch this boy play, I started thinking, no, now this can't be true, this is supposed to make me feel better, not make me realise the rest of my family is darker than me, this doesn't help at all, in fact, it makes it worse. What was I supposed to do when someone started calling me names? Turn around and say, "Well, you should see my brother; he is darker than me" No, maybe I had it wrong, perhaps I think he just looked like me because he had dark skin, so I tried not to look at him anymore, I tried to ignore the fact that he looked like me, as it may have been a boy from a different house.

And then we heard a voice from nowhere shouting.

"Get in this house now!"

My boyfriend laughed, "That's got to be your mother," he said, and I laughed too jokingly because clearly, this woman shouted like you see on the comedy shows.

Only to notice that the boy in the street who looked like me walked into Pamela's house. Oh my God, he really might be my brother; that voice must have come from Pamela's house. No - all these things aren't happening like I wanted them to. So now I knew someone was definitely in the house. So, we pulled up to the cul de sac right behind Pamela's house and I got out of the car.

"What are you doing?" said my boyfriend.

"Nothing," I said.

You could see the back of Pamela's house through a fence at the end of this Cul de Sac. So, I tried to find a small hole in what would be the fence at the back of her back garden, to try and peek through. I could see there was a line of washing, so I was curious to see what her back garden looked like, and how clean her washing was, as this was always the sign of a good mother. But I couldn't find a hole big enough or anything to climb on to peer into her garden. This was ridiculous, but I was determined to keep coming back every day until I caught even a tiny glimpse of what my real mother looked like. Although, I still definitely didn't want to meet her. I did want to see what she looked like.

Two weeks had passed, and we didn't catch a glimpse of Pamela or anyone else coming or going. During these weeks, my boyfriend and I split up for good. The abuse was too much, both physical and verbal. His parting words were, "I don't want to be with a Paki; no one will."

But I continued my stakeout at Pamela's house, only now I could stay a few hours longer, without my boyfriend moaning. After that, I went back there every day I could, sometimes late into the night. There were various comings and goings, but I didn't see anyone with blonde hair which I thought could be her.

It was 10:30 on a Sunday night. I had a modelling job the next day. So, after spending the afternoon staking out Pamela's house, I needed to get in the bath and make sure my hair had been washed and conditioned well. Then I heard a knock on the door - who on earth could that be at 10:30 on a Sunday night? I didn't tell people where I lived, so the only person it could have been was my ex-boyfriend, so I didn't answer. They knocked again, but it was too soft a knock for it to be him. My front door was at the side of my house, so I couldn't even peek through the window to see who it was, so I waited for them to go. And then I heard something being pushed through the letterbox. When the coast was clear, I picked up the piece of paper pushed through the door and opened it.

'Hello Susan, if it is you sitting outside Pamela's house, could you please let her know, as some of the neighbours are going to report a suspicious car hanging around by the school. There had been reports of people trying to abduct kids from the school. Or please call me. Signed Mary Woods.'

Oh my God!! What!! I thought with my hair dripping wet. I was completely panicked. I didn't even notice a school close by in the street. I definitely was not trying to abduct kids. I didn't know what to do, but I certainly didn't want to be arrested by the police. And with sheer panic, I jumped in my car and drove to Pamela's house. My heart is racing, but the thought of being arrested by the police for trying to abduct children far outweighed my fear of seeing Pamela.

As I knocked on the front door, I could hear voices inside, it was late, but I was scared. The door partially opened, as it seemed a little stuck. And there she stood, a blonde woman with one small child in her arms, and the boy from the street standing behind her.

"Who is it?" I heard him say.

"Pamela?" I said, querying to check if this was really her.

"Yes," she replied.

I felt numb. This was the moment I never thought would happen, there was so much to take in, but nothing was going in at all.

"Do you know who I am?" I asked.

"Yes," she replied, "but I don't know which one you are."

What??? I thought, but then I remembered she had given another child away too.

"I am Susan," I said.

"Hello," she said again.

"Do you want to come in?" she asked.

"OK," I said.

With that, I was inside my birth mother's house.

"Who is it?" the boy from the street kept asking.

"Never you mind" said Pamela. "Get to bed," she told him as we walked into her living room.

"Have a seat," she said "do you want a drink?"

"No, thank you", I replied.

I found myself just staring at her. It was one of the most surreal moments of my life. To look at someone with the same bone structure as I had, the same shaped eyes, the same features, I could see myself in her. Only she had white skin and blonde hair. These were the things that so many other people just take for granted growing up, with parents that look similar to you. And having people say things like 'ooh, she has your eyes' or 'you have the same nose', but I never had that. I couldn't stop looking at her; all the questions and anger I felt in the social worker's office had gone. I was totally unprepared for this; I hadn't planned it at all; of course, I hadn't. I didn't know people were trying to abduct kids from the local school. It felt like I'd been staring at her for hours, whereas in reality, it was probably only a few minutes, all those years with so many questions, and yet I had nothing coming out my mouth.

Then Pamela said, "How are you?"

"Fine," I replied, and I told her about the note that had been pushed through my door.

"Sorry it's so late," I said ", I've been sitting outside for a couple weeks now."

"I know," she replied.

What? I thought all those days of sitting outside thinking I was like a policeman on a stakeout, and she knew I was there all the time.

"I was going to come over to," she said, "but I didn't know if that's what you wanted."

No, it wasn't what I wanted, it definitely wasn't what I wanted, I don't want to meet you, but I wanted to see, you gave me away, I don't like you, why would I want you to come over to me? These were the thoughts going around in my head but out of my mouth came "I didn't know what to do. I didn't know if you would want to see me," I said.

"Yes," she replied, "I called the social looking for you, but they wouldn't tell me anything; they're only allowed to tell the child about the mothers and not the other way around."

So, you were trying to look for me first? I thought, so you must have thought about me for all these years? Maybe you're not the big bad wolf after all? I thought. No words were coming out of my mouth; I was totally caught off guard.

"Did your parents look after you, OK," she asked?

"Yes, they did." I replied.

I couldn't sit down and tell her my parents were too strict, and I ran away from home, and it's all your fault because you gave me away. However, looking at her house, it wasn't much better than the house I grew up in, so if I had been brought up here, things might have been the same.

"Do you know about your sister?" she asked.

"I know about her, but I've never met her," I said, "I have a brother, don't I?"

"Yes, you have three," she said.

"Three?" I replied, surprised, as I only knew about one. So we are like the bloody Von Trapps now.

"You have an older brother called Terry," she said.

"Terry?" I said, "I thought it was Tilly; it said Tilly on my paperwork."

She laughed "No, Terry and there's also Richard and Daniel" she said, pointing to the two kids sitting on the stairs listening.

"OK," I said, "so you're not with my father anymore?" I asked.

"No," we split up before Emma was born.

"Why did you give me away?" I asked.

"I didn't want to; it was Tony's fault, but we had no money, we couldn't afford to keep you, but I did think about you all of the time," I could see her mouth moving, but the words weren't sinking into my head.

"Have you heard from him? Do you know where he is?" I asked.

"No, I haven't heard from him or know anything about him since back then," she said.

We did continue to chat for a while, but I don't remember much about the conversation. I'm not sure whether I have blocked it out or because everything was a blur; it didn't sink in, but I left Pamela's house quite late that night.

Her parting words were, "will I see you again?"

"Yes," I said, I will be in touch."

"OK," she replied, "it was nice to meet you."

"You too," I said. And with that, I drove away from the home of my birth mother.

I didn't see Pamela again or try to contact her. I couldn't fathom how I felt, I still had unanswered questions, and most importantly, I still didn't know what my father looked like. It was surreal to see my birth mother and to see my facial features in her, but at the same time, it wasn't enough. It didn't tell me anything. She was white. I don't have a problem with my white side. But, the brown side of me caused most of the issues in my life.

A few months later, it was Mother's Day; of course, I would send my mom a Mother's Day card; this was the first year I had two mothers. I wasn't sure if I would ever see Pamela again, but I did know she was my birth mother, and I did know where she lived, so I got her a Mother's Day card too and pushed it through her letterbox. I didn't think much of it, as it might have mainly been for her benefit more than mine. Then I had a letter asking for me to call Mary Woods. I didn't know what she wanted to speak to me about, had something happened to Pamela? Or maybe she had news about my sister, I didn't know but, still being the curious person that I was, I called her.

"I understand you've met Pamela", she said.

"Yes," I replied.

"How did it go?" She asked.

"I don't know," I said and told her what had happened.

"Well, Pamela has been in touch with me, she told me you had sent her a Mother's Day card, and this meant so much to her, but she's not heard, or seen you since," Mary said.

"I know," I said, "she's not my mom. My mom is the one that brought me up and looked after me. So, I don't know how I feel about Pamela. I didn't know she wanted to see me again. She could have looked for me if she was really that bothered over the years; we hadn't moved house," I said.

"I probably shouldn't tell you this," said Mary, "but, I am retiring soon, I was a social worker at the time when they put you up for adoption back in 1970, and she didn't want to give you up, not really. But when you called me early on this year, saying you were looking for Pamela, well, she had also called me that very same day. I thought someone was playing a joke on me because I couldn't believe after 21 years, the mother and the daughter would contact me on exactly the same day; it was really spooky. It was the spookiest thing I had ever experienced," Mary said.

I couldn't believe what I was hearing, "you never said anything?" I said. "I wasn't allowed to; that was why I was trying to convince you to give her a chance. She was heartbroken when she gave you up, I think it was more Tony's idea than Pamela's, but now she's told me how happy she was that you knocked on her door the other month, and she understands if you don't want to see her again."

The hatred I had towards this seemingly evil woman for giving up not one, but two of her children was huge. But what if she really was a nice woman who made a mistake because she loved Tony so much? But she still did it, I thought, I was so conflicted in my head.

"Maybe if you write to her, or I could get in touch with her, and we can arrange a meeting, the three of us here in my office, and talk it through. All I know is that she loves you, and she would love to be part of your life," said Mary.

"I don't know", I said, but in my head, I thought, I don't want to sit in a room and have a conversation with two effective strangers to me. I would feel like I was being forced to like someone.

"I don't know what to do," I said again to Mary.

"Well, I will leave it with you," Mary said, "I'll be retiring in a couple of weeks, and I would love for you two to have a happy ending."

I didn't know how to feel, I didn't know whether to feel happy, knowing that my birth mother wasn't all that bad. After all she came looking for me, and it was really spooky that we both made the same call the same day, some might say it was meant to be. But then there were still so many unanswered questions, and I still felt angry that because of Tony and Pamela, I had and still have so much abuse and hatred towards me. But no one could understand. No one knew what it felt like to be me, or knew what it felt like to not be wanted as a baby, no one knew what it felt like to be adopted, and certainly, no one knew what it was like to live in a racist world looking like me, no one.

Except for possibly one person. Emma, my real sister.

CHAPTER THIRTEEN

Sister act

Emma Michelle, and Wombourne - that's all I knew. My real sister's name was Emma Michelle something, and she went to a family in Wombourne. So armed with that knowledge, I went to the main library in town and returned to the electoral rolls, and I looked up every single Emma Michelle in the whole village; there couldn't be that many, and that's what I did. I spent an entire week researching and relentlessly searching through the electoral rolls for that area, looking for anyone called Emma or Emma Michelle, regardless of the surname.

The electoral rolls only have names; they don't have dates of birth. And some only have the first and last names, no middle names. So, all I could do was write down on a piece of paper every single person called Emma Michelle and anyone called just Emma who lived in Wombourne.

I had 365 names and addresses, now which one of these was my real sister? I was also aware that her name may have been changed completely. There was only one way to find out for sure. With lists of potential sisters, I headed off to the village itself.

I had to knock on every single door on this list to try and find my real sister, the only person in the whole world who could have any understanding of what my life has been like.

And so it began, "Hello, are you, Emma Michelle?" I would ask.

"Yes", one replied. I could clearly see this wasn't my Emma as this person was a white woman who looked about 60, and I knew Emma would only be two years younger than me.

"I'm so sorry, I'm looking for someone, this is the wrong house." I would say.

Some people were not in at all. And sometimes I asked if an Emma Michelle was living there.

Some would say, "yes, but she's not here right now."

Then I would ask, "Is she around my age and does she look like me?" "No," they would say, then I would be on to the next one.

Some were more difficult than others, so I would have to tell them that I was adopted and looking for my real sister. Some people responded with, "no, this definitely isn't the house", safe in the knowledge that they didn't have a brown skin person in their family.

Six days it took me to knock on almost all the doors, some I had to return back to if no one was in. If I couldn't get an answer, I would knock on the neighbour's door and ask if a girl living next door looked like me. I had to get through the list. I had to find her. I knew she was there somewhere.

It was a Friday afternoon, and it had poured with rain. I'd had no joy of finding Emma. I had one house left to go; it was at the end of a long road and looked quite prominent. I knocked on the door, and there was no reply, so I went next door.

"Hello, do you know if there is a Emma who lives next door?"

"Yes," said the man who had opened the door.

"OK," I said, "does she have dark hair, around my age, does she look a bit like me?"

"I'm not sure," he said, "a little bit. I don't know."

Well, that's no help at all, I thought.

"I was adopted, and I'm looking for my real sister. I've knocked on 364 houses, and this is the last house I can try," I told him, "Are you sure she doesn't look like me?" I implored.

"Maybe a little bit, but she will be back home soon; maybe you can wait?" he said, trying to be helpful.

"Oh, OK," I said, "Thank you for your help", and I walked back to my car.

This was my last house and my last hope, although I didn't have much hope at all. There were some garages opposite this man's house, so I parked my car and sat and waited, I had nothing left to lose, so I might as well hang on until they came home from work.

I didn't have to wait that long; half an hour I saw a bright yellow Skoda pull onto the drive, with teddy bears in the back window. Oh my God, I thought, trust me to have a sister driving around in a custard coloured Skoda. But as this was the last house, I waited to see who got out. Then, finally, a young girl got out of the vehicle. Ooh, I don't know, I thought, she does have dark hair and looked around my age, but she's a lot paler than I am, but I will still go and ask the question anyway. So I got out of my car and caught her before she actually walked into the house.

"Excuse me, I'm sorry to bother you, are you, Emma Michelle?" I asked.

"I'm Emma," she said.

"Oh, I'm sorry, I must have the wrong house," I said as I turned to walk away, feeling defeated.

"Why?" she asked.

I turned around, so as we stood on her driveway in the pouring rain, I explained, "It's OK, I'm adopted, and I know I have a sister, and I'm looking for her. All I know is a name is either Emma or Emma Michelle, I don't know the surname, I've knocked on all these houses and yours was the last one. I'm so sorry to have bothered you."

"No, it's not me," she said, "You've got the wrong house."

"OK, sorry," and I walked away feeling deflated down her drive to get in my car.

She went into her house and shut the door. I started my engine. I had to just accept I will probably never, ever find out who my real sister is. I will never meet the only other person in the whole world that may have experienced a life similar to mine, a life where I never felt I belonged, and a life of not knowing who I really was, but at least I tried, I tried so hard. As I looked over my shoulder to pull onto the road, I saw the young girl I had just spoken to running towards me. "Stop!" she shouted.

I wound my window down, and she approached the car.

"You haven't got the wrong house," she said, "it's me, I'm Emma, and

I'm adopted too," she said.

"What?" I replied, "How old are you?"

"19," she said.

It was her, it had to be her, but her hair was much darker than mine, and she had a slightly different facial structure, but highly similar at the same time, it's her, it's got to be her, I thought. But hang on, she's white, a funny kind of white, but she's kind of white.

"Would you like to come in?" she asked.

"OK," I said.

She looked very posh, nothing like me, her skirt was past her knees for a start. Did she look like me? Yes? No? So we walked into her house and into the kitchen, where we sat down at the table.

"I'm not sure if I have the right person," I said.

I continued to tell her my story.

"What do you know? I asked.

She said, "I didn't know I was adopted, until recently, when I went looking in my mom's drawers for my birth certificate so I could apply for a driver's license. And that's when I found papers saying I was adopted. Hold on."

She went upstairs and came back down with some photographs. They were pictures of her when she was really young. I picked up the photos, and if I hadn't have seen her fetch them with my own eyes, I would have thought that they were pictures of me; when I was younger, we looked like we could have been twins. We looked exactly the same; we even had the same T-bar shoes on and stroppy looking expressions on our faces. This was actually my real sister!!

Emma had no idea she had a sister; she didn't have the information like I had. And there was a moment when time seemed to stop just for a tiny minute when we realised we were indeed sisters.

I asked her what her childhood was like.

"Great," she said, "My mom and dad couldn't have children, so they adopted two boys and me," she said, "but it was brilliant; they really loved me."

I could feel it in that house, it was a house full of love, a big beautiful house, why didn't I go to a big posh family in Wombourne. I thought. "What was your childhood like?" she asked.

"It was OK," I said, "it wasn't great, but it was OK."

I can't explain the feeling I had talking to her, and looking at her, it was something I had never felt before; it felt so surreal. It was almost like an invisible kind of umbilical cord between us, linking us together.

Then I heard someone come through the door, it was her mom.

"Hello," I said as this lady walked into the room.

"Hello," she replied, with a big friendly smile on her face.

"Mom, this is Susan," Emma said.

"Hello," repeated her mom.

Wow, her mom was so utterly different from mine, I thought.

"Susan is my real sister," Emma said without a blink of an eye.

"Oh, nice to meet you," her mom said.

I felt a little bit awkward as I didn't want her mom to think I had come to steal away my sister.

"I should go," I said as I got my things together.

"OK," said Emma, "well, let's keep in touch," she said.

We swapped telephone numbers and promised to see each other again. That was it. I now had a real sister, of course. I still had my adopted sister, but I hadn't seen her for a while; she had left home and had a child of her own, her own life. She was a lot older than me. Emma was different. Everything felt different.

Emma and I became inseparable. It was astonishing how alike we were; we would finish each other's sentences, we would laugh at the same things, we used to turn up to meet each other in almost the same clothes (Emma's skirts were getting shorter). I'd never experienced anything like this ever, and it felt so good. We were with each other almost every day, we started going out clubbing and doing all the things which young girls do. I told her I had met Pamela, but she had no interest at all in meeting her, and why would she? She didn't need to look for answers. She grew up blessed; she grew up within a really loving family. She didn't need to look for anything missing because there wasn't anything missing in her life. Because her skin was slightly paler than mine, she didn't have as much bullying as I did.

We used to go out all of the time, and we were proud to introduce ourselves to people as sisters. However, we had to deal with racist comments from people, mainly because people could see we were related, even though our colour was slightly different.

I wasn't allowed around Emma's house; her parents didn't really like us being together. Emma told me that she thought her parents thought she didn't love them so much anymore because I was in her life, and they worried that she would leave them for me. So, once again, I found myself being the secret, not friend or partner this time, but the secret sister, but a secret nonetheless.

I was kind of OK with this because what Emma and I had together was beautiful and meant the world to me. We were having the time of our lives, and I loved her so much; I finally had someone in my life that knew everything about me and still loved me; she didn't care how I looked or about the colour of my skin, or the fact I was adopted. Life was great.

Well, life was great when we were together, when we weren't, everything was the same, boyfriends still calling me a Paki, people in the street were still calling me names, and I was still being judged on the colour of my skin at work. Emma was part of this world too now, so together, we started denying who we were and telling people that we were Italian or Spanish and sometimes even Chinese! But that didn't stop the curiosity; that didn't stop the unanswered questions of why we were given away. Despite what Pamela had told me, it seemed she was the innocent party and just went along with what Tony wanted. So, I still needed to know the facts. I still needed to see the cold-hearted person that just threw me away. But now, it wasn't just me. It was Emma too, we had to meet our father.

CHAPTER FOURTEEN

Inconvenience Store

Jaswant Singh Kanth. Or as I preferred to call him Tony, his English name.

Where was I to even start? I remembered Pamela telling me that he owned an off license on the main road out of town. Great, off I went there, as it's a shop, it's a public place so I could just walk in.

As I pulled up outside the shop, I looked up, 'Kanth Stores' in Big Blue letters. I just sat there looking up at this sign out of my car window in big, bold letters, that was his name, that was my name. I had been past this shop so often and to think my real father might be inside. So, feeling brave, I thought I would just go in buy something and see what the shop was like, if it was tidy, clean and all those kinds of things. I didn't know if he worked behind the counter, or if he would know who I was instantly. It had been 21 years since I was born; surely birth parents have that kind of invisible connection you just know you are related too.

There was only one way to find out. It was pretty dull inside as I walked into the shop; every shelf was tightly packed with produce. I had a little look at everything on the shelves, and it didn't seem anything special, just like any ordinary shop that we saw every day. As I walked around the store, I tried to look at the people behind the counter, who were already staring at me. Oh, they must know, I must have one of those post-it notes on my forehead, which states, yes, I am Tony's daughter. There were two people behind the counter who were staring at me and whispering to each other. They had to know, it's true, there really is one of those invisible family ties, almost like a smell that animals have when they recognise each other.

They watched every movement I made around the shop for about 5 to 10 minutes, it was then I realised that I was watching them. Oh no, they must have thought I was a shoplifter! So I approached the counter and picked up some chewing gum to buy. It was then it seemed like they were staring right through me, right into my soul, with some kind of recognition, but I didn't say a thing; I just smiled. Did they know? Did they somehow recognise me? Could they read my mind? Could this be my aunt or uncle? Maybe even my brother or sister? They were clearly too young to be Tony.

"Thank you," I said, as they handed me my change, I left the shop and jumped back in my car.

I sat there for a few moments trying to decipher in my head images of their faces and mentally trying to establish if they looked like me. They kind of did, they kind of looked just like me, or did I think that just because they had dark hair, brown skin and brown eyes? Or was I seeing that because I needed to? I just made myself even more confused. I didn't feel satisfied. I had to go back in.

As I went back into the shop, they were already looking at me as I walked through the door. So, they must know, I thought.

"Hello, is Tony in?" I asked.

"Pardon," they said.

"Tony, is Tony here?"

"No," they both said in unison while smiling.

They are lying, I thought. I can tell by how they were smiling and yet still staring at me; they were trying to cover for him; they know, they must know. Or maybe they didn't use his English name, so I tried again.

"Jaswant, Jaswant Singh Kanth," I said.

"No," they replied.

Are they lying, or did they know I was his secret child, and they were trying to protect him? I thought. I knew they knew something, so I pressed.

"Tony, Tony," I repeated as I pointed to the shop sign despite it being outside, "The person who owns this shop, your boss," I said. "Tony, Tony, Jaswant?"

They looked at each other, said something in their own language, and repeated it back to me.

"Jaswant?"

"Yes," I replied.

"No," they said, "not here."

"When will he be back?" I asked, "Where is he?"

"Don't know, not here," was the reply.

"OK, do you have a telephone number for him, please?"

They look at each other, and I asked again. This time I used my hands to signwriting on a piece of paper, "telephone number," I said. "No, no", they replied.

"You do not have a telephone number for your boss?" I asked.

I was getting annoyed as it felt like they clearly knew something but didn't want to say. They said something to each other again which I could not understand, then they scribbled down a number on a piece of paper and passed it to me. It was a landline number but no name.

"What's this?" I asked. "Is this his telephone number? Is this his home number?"

"Yes, yes," they said.

"Where is it?" I asked.

"Wells Road, 146 Wells Road," they said.

"That's his home address?" I asked.

"Yes," they replied.

"OK, thank you."

And with that, I left the shop and got back in my car.

Wells Rd was a continuation of the road I was already on; it was one of the main roads out of the town towards the nearest village. So, I drove over the island and continued up Wells Road, looking for number 146. Looking out of the window, 140, 142, 144, 148, I couldn't see a 146; this was the corner of the street, and the house on the opposite corner of the road was 148. So, I was confused. I parked the car and got out.

I walked up and down the section of the road; still no sign of 146. I looked at the side of the houses, behind all the places I could and nothing. It jumped from 144 to 148. The only thing in the middle was a Sikh temple. I looked again and again and again. No definitely nothing, well, except a Sikh temple in the middle of 144 and 148.

And then the penny dropped, and once again, I found myself with similar feelings to that I had standing on the motorway bridge in Stafford upon receiving my original birth certificate. Number 146 was a Sikh temple! 146 was my father's home! Could my life of gotten much worse? My father's home was a fucking temple! What was the point? What was the fucking point of me carrying on this search? All it seems to be bringing me is more heartache and pain? I feel like the more I find out, the deeper down in a big black hole, I seemed to be sinking!

I went back into my car and just stared out the window; I thought this is ridiculous, but I knew I had to continue my quest. I also knew there was no way I would knock on the door of a temple. So, I headed off to the nearest phone box to call the number the shop gave me. With a purse full of change, I dialled the number and inserted my coins.

"***," someone said as the receiver was picked up.

"Hello," I said.

"***" they repeated.

I had no idea what they said. I could not understand. I knew it wasn't English; of course, it wasn't.

In typical British fashion, I repeated. "Hello," but in a louder voice, thinking that would make me better understood.

"Hello," someone replied.

Finally, I thought, "Is Tony there?" I asked.

"***," they replied.

Again, I still could not understand what they said, so I asked the same question only slightly louder.

I heard the person on the other end of the phone talking to someone else.

"Jaswant, Jaswant, Singh, Kanth," I shouted.

Still, I heard voices on the other end of the phone of them talking to each other, then the receiver was then passed someone else.

"Hello," they said.

"Hello, hello, I'm looking for Tony, Jaswant Singh Kanth. Is he there?" I said, frustrated.

"Tony" they said.

"Yes," I replied.

"No, he is not here; who is it?" they replied.

Frustratingly I persisted. "I need to speak to him." I said.

"Who are you?" they asked.

"I need to speak to him. I'm Susan," I said.

"Who?" they asked.

"Susan," I didn't really care anymore, "I am his daughter; where is he?"

"Oh, oh, he's not here."

"When will he be there?" I asked.

"Call tomorrow," she said and put the phone down.

I was fuming. I didn't know if they understood what I was saying or just covering for him. Maybe they just thought I was prank calling, so I called the number back.

"Hello," I said, "where is Tony?" I asked as slowly and clearly as I possibly could.

The same person answered and just said, "Call back tomorrow, tomorrow," and put the phone down again.

Frustrated, I knew I wouldn't get anywhere, so I exited the phone box and returned to the phone box the following day, I redialled the number.

"I called yesterday. Is Tony there?" I asked.

This time, a man answered, and I could hear people talking in the background; it sounded like a few people were around the handset. "Hello, hello," he said.

"Hello, I am looking for Tony, for Jaswant," I said.

"He isn't here," said the man.

"When will he be there? I need to speak to him."

"I don't know - who is it?" asked the man.

I was still frustrated from the day before, and I could feel myself getting angry again, as I had visions of a brick wall in front of me as usual. "I am his daughter," I said, "and I need to see him."

"He is not here," said the man, "he's coming up the weekend, I think."

"What do you mean?" I asked, "Does he not live there?"

"No, London, he lives in London," said the man.

"London?" I said. "But he's coming up on Saturday?"

"Yes, I think," said the man.

"You think? You either know, or you don't, if he is coming," I said, feeling like they were deliberately being evasive.

"I don't know, I don't know," he replied.

I lost all my patience, and as I already had zero respect for him, I said, "He gave me away 21 years ago, and I want to see him, so I will call again Saturday morning, and if he is not there, I will happily come around there and tell everyone what he did."

I must have had my big girl pants on because I don't know where that came from, except it must have been born out of frustration, anger, fear, rejection, and many other things.

"Yes," said the man.

I just slammed the phone down.

I had arranged to see Emma later that day; I told her what I had said. She thought it was amusing. And despite not really caring about meeting him or Pamela, we agreed we would meet him together, assuming he actually came up, that is. And then our minds started going all over the place. What if he kidnaped us? What if we ended up being one of those honour killings that you hear about on the news? What if he drove us to the temple and locks us in there, and we were subjected to all kinds of depravity for being the shameful children he had many moons ago? We ended up scaring ourselves, but we were adamant we wanted to see him. I think we still wanted to see where we both really came from. We still wanted to see the person we blamed for my life of shit.

Saturday Morning came around and I picked Emma up at the corner of her street so her parents wouldn't see who she was with. We drove to a phone box and called Tony's house again. There was no reply; Emma and I looked at each other, "The bastard, he can't just ignore us," we said.

"I'm going to try again, as the phone rang and rang; eventually, someone picked up.

"Hello," I said. There was silence. "Hello," I said, a little louder.

"Hello," said a young girl, well she sounded about 20.

"Is Tony there?" I asked.

"No," said the girl.

"Where is he?" I asked. "Doesn't he want to see us? We are his daughters?"

"Yes," said the girl.

"Yes, he will see us?" I asked.

Now I wasn't sure if she just didn't understand what I was trying to say.

"Where is he?" I asked.

"He's not getting here until 12:30," she said.

"OK, will he see us? Does he know I have called?"

"Yes," said the girl.

"He will see us?" I was trying to get clarity.

"Yes, where?" asked the girl.

I was flummoxed, "OK, ask him to meet us outside the church in town at 1pm, please."

"OK, yes," said the girl.

"I had my big girl pants on again, and I said, "If he is not there, I will come around to his house."

"He will be there," said the girl.

"OK, great."

And with that, I replaced the receiver and turned to Emma, who had her ear next to the handset the whole time. We just looked at each other, and I said, “I bet he doesn’t turn up.”

“What if he wants to kill us?” Emma said; at that moment, the adrenaline had turned to panic and fear and wonder.

“I will phone Nigel,” said Emma, “and get him to come with us.”

Nigel was Emma’s boyfriend and was quite tall, so hopefully, with a male presence with us, nothing would go wrong.

CHAPTER FIFTEEN

Tony

We sat in Nigel's Nissan Micra outside the church, it was just before 12:30 as we wanted to get there a little earlier so he could not say he turned up and we were not there. Emma and I got out the car and waited by the church wall.

Every single person that walked past, everyone that stopped and looked around, we squinted trying to decide, is that him? Had he got brown hair? Tick, had he got brown eyes? Brown skin? Could he look a little bit like us? Then as the person gets closer it would become clear it was not Tony, they would either be in their 20s or there would be some other reason. Emma and I were anxious in anticipation, what if he drove up in a big Rolls Royce, or a huge van that he used to go to the cash and carry for his shop? Or he may even turn up on a bicycle for all we knew. After all he did own a business, seemed to come from a big family and he lived in London, so maybe he would be wearing a suit or dressed head to toe in designer wear.

It was 1:00 pm, and there was no sign of him, or indeed anyone who could be anything like him, of course he was not coming. Who turns up to meet someone who says they are your daughter? we could have been anyone. Emma and I felt such an anticlimax, disappointed and hurt, which soon started to turn to anger, making us feel like he had abandoned us all over again.

"What now?" Emma said.

"I don't know," I replied, but being young and feisty as I was, I said, "right, let us go around to that temple or we could go into the shop and just refuse to leave until he comes."

As we turned to walk towards Nigel's car a silver, scruffy looking car pulled up and wound down the window.

"Tony?" I questioned whilst peering in to the car.

" Yes" he said.

"Where shall we go?" I asked.

"I don't know," he replied.

Just relieved at the fact that he turned up, we were not going to question or push things at this point, but we knew we were not going to pass up this opportunity to find some answers. I looked at Emma. "Hold on," she said as she walked over to Nigel who was sitting waiting patiently in his car.

I just stood staring at Tony, he had dark hair, and brown eyes, not very skinny but quite tidy in his dress, I tried to look for any signs of anything in his eyes.

Emma returned to the car and said to me, "Nigel is going to follow us, just in case."

"Ok, great," I said, thinking that way if he decided to kidnap us, or kill us, Nigel could come in like a superhero to the rescue.

Emma and I sat in the back of Tony's car, that way it would have been harder for him to club us over the head.

"How are you?" I asked.

"I am fine," he replied.

I was trying to absorb everything about him in my head, this was my father, my real father, he existed, he had lovely hair, clean shaven but did not seem that tall, but this was also the person that gave me away, the cold hearted, callous, despicable person who left me at social services as a 3-month-old baby. I looked down at his feet. He did not have any shoes on! He had slip on grey shoes which he had taken off and they were pushed by his seat. I could not believe he was driving around with bare feet. We were driving around in circles and going nowhere.

I looked at Emma and whispered. "Where are we going?"

She shook her head in a kind of, 'I have no idea' manner.

"Where are we going?" I asked Tony.

Just driving around, he said.

I looked at Emma again. Flabbergasted.

"Can't we go to a pub or a café?" I asked.

What for? He replied.

Shocked, I said" So, we can sit and just talk."

"What about?" he replied.

My eyes must have popped out my head, but trying to keep calm I repeated, "We could just find somewhere to sit and talk, like a café or something."

"Well, do you have any money?" He asked.

I looked back at Emma. With a look of did he just say that?

"Pardon?" I said.

"Well, what do you want?" He asked in a questionable manner.

I could not believe my ears. "What do you mean? What do I want? We are your daughters."

"But we gave you up, for someone else to have, so I don't know what you want." Tony replied.

I felt like my breath had been ripped away. I did not expect this. I did not expect, that someone who could give up a baby to question why we wanted to find him? To genuinely be so cold that he could think giving us up would just close that chapter in his life like it never happened. Surely that's like giving away a piece of furniture that you do not want anymore, to never think about it again.

I was dumbstruck, "What? Have you never even thought about us at all? I asked.

"No," Tony replied with a quick clean sharp retort.

This could not be real life, this could not be happening, I thought. I do not know if I felt angry or hurt.

"I was your first ever child, are you telling me you have not once thought in 21 years - oh I wonder how she is or what she looks like, nothing, nothing at all?"

"No, we gave you up," he said in a way that he could not believe that we were surprised he could think that way.

At that moment I just felt numb, I did not expect that at all. I was prepared to call him all the names under the sun and to get angry with him, I was prepared for him to feel remorseful, I was even prepared for him to apologise for his horrendous behaviour back in 1970. But I was not prepared for someone, not just anyone, but our real father to question what we wanted. I did not know whether I wanted to cry, scream, or punch him in the head, I looked at Emma dumbfounded. Emma said to him, "why did you give us up?"

He looked at Emma through the rear-view mirror, "I didn't give you up" he said.

"Yes, you did," Emma replied.

"No, not you," he said to Emma, "that was Pam."

"You gave us both up," I said, "you took us to social services and left us there."

"No, you are not mine," he said to Emma.

Tony's name was not on Emma's birth certificates.

"Yes, you are," I said to him, "why did you have us, if you did not want us?"

"It was not me," he said, "it was Pamela."

"No, she told us it was your idea, she didn't know anything, you just took me and left me at social services," I said.

"No, no we both did, we both decided we would give you up" he protested.

"That's not true, I've met Pamela, and she told me everything. She said it was all you, it was your idea not hers, she didn't want to do it." I implored.

"No, no, no, that is not true," he said.

I saw him starting to get a little angry, this made us wonder if Pam was lying. What if he was telling us the truth and Pamela was just covering her own back all along, she had made me believe that Tony was the instigator, Tony was the big bad wolf and it was all Tony's idea. But it did not feel like she was lying when I met her, it felt like she was telling me the truth. Why did she try to find me if it was her idea to give me away in the first place? I thought.

This was not working out as we thought it would, we did not have the answers we thought we wanted. In fact, we had even more questions, but still feeling resentful towards Tony I said, "No, you are a liar, how could you do that? How could you give up your first child?"

"No, no we both did, it was a joint decision," he replied.

We were still driving around the streets; Nigel carried on following in the car behind us. There we were in a car with our real father, and all we could actually see of him was his eyes in a rear-view mirror. Was he telling the truth? Was Pamela the devil in disguise? Was he Emma's father? So many thoughts were going through my head. Or maybe he was lying through his teeth because he did not want any trouble, he did not want his big secret coming out so I asked him "Are you married now?"

"Yes," he replied "I have a wife."

"Do you have any children?"

"Yes," he said "five."

"Five children - so you give away your first two and you went on to have five more? And yet you still say you never gave us a thought in all these years? Do they know about us?" I asked.

"Me and my wife we have no secrets," he said.

Maybe he was a changed man, maybe he really is the good cop out of him and Pamela. After all he is a businessman, seemed successful, and it seemed he had a happy ever after marriage plus five children, so I asked him "okay, if you and your wife have no secrets when did you tell her about us?"

"Yesterday," he replied.

Well, Emma and I fell about laughing.

"So, you and your wife have no secrets, but you only told her about us yesterday, after 21 years?" I said.

"Yes" he replied, not seeing the irony.

"You are full of shit," I said.

I felt like we had exposed him for being a liar and keeping the secret of having two other children from his wife until the day before meeting us, meant everything that came out of his mouth was not to be trusted.

"So, why are you blaming Pamela for giving us up when it was you? It was you all along, it was all your idea you did not want us two." I said.

"No, no that is not true, we both discussed, and we both agreed," he was starting to get annoyed.

As much as I was angry at him part of me could see the genuine frustration in his face and tone of voice. Who was lying? One of them must be lying, not that it made too much of a difference, but if only we knew the truth, if only we knew which one of them was the one who left us at social services. Which one of them suggested the idea to give up their children, to give them away, then we would know which one is to blame. We would know which one to hate more. There was only one way to find out. We must get Pamela and Tony face to face.

Right - I thought feeling all strong and driven by frustration "When was the last time you spoke to Pamela?" I asked Tony.

"Not since we split up," he said.

"Nothing? Not even when you knew we were looking for you?" I asked thinking they may have concocted some kind of plan between them to get their story straight, albeit they weren't so straight after all.

"Nothing, nothing at all," Tony replied. "Nothing, I have not spoken to her since we split up" he said.

Again, who knew if that was true or not, we could not believe a word that came out this man's mouth, he had held onto this secret for 21 years, even through a second marriage and 5 children. He is a liar, and completely capable of lying to us.

"Well, why are you blaming Pamela for everything?" I asked.

"Because it's true," he said.

"Well, we'll soon see who is telling the truth, take this next left," I said "I'm taking you to Pamela's house, to see if you will say that to her face."

"OK," he said.

Wow, I thought, surely, he would not want a confrontation with Pamela in front of us if he was not confident in what he was saying. Maybe he thought we would not put them both together? Was he calling our bluff? At this point we really did not give a shit what he thought we just wanted to know the truth. I turned to Emma and asked if she would be okay if we drove to Pamela's house and get them both together.

"Yes, that's fine," she said, she was angry too, and did not care, she just wanted to expose Tony for the liar he was.

This would be the first time I had seen Pamela since we met, and since I sent her the Mother's Day card. Once again it was a surprise visit, but driven by a quest for the truth, peppered with the need to humiliate Tony and back him into a corner, exposing him for the lying, cold, horrendous, person we thought he was. I continued to direct him to Pamela's house.

We pulled up outside Pamela's house, and I got out the car, I told Emma to stay in the car thinking she would stop Tony from driving away. I looked at Nigel who had pulled up behind us, he looked at me as if to ask if everything was OK and I nodded to confirm it was fine. I knocked on Pamela's front door, with a huge sense of Déjà vu - the adrenaline had been going through my body so rapidly.

Pamela answered the door, her face lit up, "Hello," she said with a smile on her face.

"Hello" I said "We have just met Tony."

"Okay," she said.

"And he is blaming you for everything, Emma is in the car also," I said. "What do you mean?" she replied confused.

"He said it was all your idea to give us away."

"No, it wasn't, he is lying, it was him, it was all his idea," she said.

"Well, can you come and say that to his face? Because we are not getting the truth, you are just blaming each other," I asked.

"Yes," she said with no hesitation.

I walked back to the car, at this point we did not give a thought to how it must have felt for Pamela and Tony seeing each other again after over 20 years. Maybe that was a bit selfish or inconsiderate of us, but we were fed up of hitting brick walls and lies. We just wanted answers, we just wanted the truth.

"She's coming," I said.

I sat down next to Emma in the back of Tony's car feeling all smug that

Tony was going to be exposed. He was the person whose fault it was that I had had years of bullying, fighting, humiliation and belittlement, and all the rubbish that I had been through my life. He was finally going to get his comeuppance. I was finally going to feel retribution, payback, or satisfaction that he was going to feel a tiny bit of pain, tiny compared to a lifetime of abandonment and grief that I had suffered.

Pamela got in the front seat next to Tony "Hello," she said.

They greeted one another after I made the introductions. For a split second there was that moment of two ex-partners meeting again for the first time, they really did have some kind of connection. Pamela had a big smile on her face. But hold on, we were not sat there for star-crossed lovers to be reunited like Romeo and Juliet. This was not about them, it was about what they did to us.

"Tony said it was your idea to give us up," I said, "is that true?

"No," she said to Tony, "it was your idea."

Tony snapped back "no it wasn't, it was your idea."

"No, you said the family do not accept her and we needed to give her up," said Pamela.

"No, we talked about it, we didn't have anything," Tony replied "it was the best thing, you agreed."

"No, I didn't," said Pamela.

Emma and I just sat in the back watching both start to argue and blame each other, like two children fighting in a playground, back and forth.

I interrupted, "he said he is not Emma's father."

"Yes, you are," Pamela said to Tony.

Tony shook his head he said "no."

"How could you say that?" Pamela asked.

"You were sleeping with everyone," he said, "there were lots of people there."

"No, I wasn't," said Pamela, in a louder voice, "she is yours."

I interrupted again, "Well why didn't you put his name on her birth certificate?" I asked Pamela.

"Because he had disappeared by then," she said.

"No, it was because I am not the father," Tony snapped back, then, they both just started arguing between themselves again.

It was like, when you are sat in a pub with a group of friends and two of them start arguing, we just sat back and watched like a tennis game, back and forth, back, blaming each other and accusing each other. Emma and I found it a little amusing at first, until we realised, we were not getting any real answers and we were not moving forward with anything. We were none the wiser.

"Well, someone is lying," I said.

"It's him," said Pamela.
"No, no I am not lying, it's you," and then they started again!!

Until silence. Neither of them was getting anywhere, or accepting blame. Neither of them wanted to be accountable for the lives of two girls in the back of Tonys car. Pamela just looked at us, as if to ask what now?

I looked at Emma, she rolled her eyes and just said, "Let's go," she looked fed up and to be honest she was not really that interested.

I felt we had exhausted all avenues; we were never going to get to know the truth and know what really happened back in 1970. Pamela and Tony were too obstinate and stubborn to put their hands up and say they had made a mistake. But then how can someone admit to making such a huge mistake, not once but twice, that is not a mistake, that is a choice. Pamela and Tony were just sat in silence, not looking at each other, like lovers do after an argument, no one wants to be the one that speaks first.

We really were not going to get any answers, so I said "we need to leave."

And with that, Pamela got out the car, leaned back through the window, and said to Emma "it was nice to meet you."

Emma did not respond.

"I will be in touch," I said to Pamela.

"OK, sure," she replied, and she went back into her house.

As Emma and I prepared to get out of our father's car, Tony turned to face us as best he could, he was holding something in his hand.
"Can I take a picture?" he asked, as he held up a small camera, with a smile on his face.

The audacity of the man! How dare he ask or even expect a photograph of two people he did not want, and didn't even want to acknowledge! But he wanted a photograph of us, what for? We did not understand, was it to show off? 'Look I have new two grown up daughters' kind of thing? Or was it because he did really care? Or was it to hand around to his family to make sure they kept away from us? We did not know, but because we could not believe his cheek!

We turned around and said "No, you cannot take a picture."

We got out the car and never saw or heard off him again.

As we sat back in Nigel's car to drive home, Emma and I just sat in silence.

"How did you get on?" asked Nigel.

"I will tell you later," said Emma.

Emma was just fed up and just wanted to get home, or she was still trying to process like I was. My was mind was all over the place, with questions and frustration, we had no satisfaction, no clarity, no sense of relief, and certainly no answers. In fact, we had nothing! Nothing at all! I had expected to find something, anything, at least some emotional relief, upon meeting the person whom I got my darkness and foreignness from.

Maybe I would have felt better if he had turned out to be a nice person. Would I have felt better if he held his hands up to say he had regretted giving us away for his whole life? Or if he gave us a box full of birthday cards, proving that he had thought about us all of the time. Or would it be better if I knew for certain everything was his fault. If I knew he had beaten himself up every day for the past 21 years.

In contrast would I have felt better if he wanted to welcome us into his new family life? If he wanted to be a father to us now? Would we have felt better if he just told us that he loved us?

What I did know was that by meeting, nothing much had changed, my skin was still brown, the National Front were still at large and society was still racist. It seemed all the Pandora's boxes that had been opened and ready to be sealed tight upon meeting our father were nowhere near ready to close. They were still very much open with no sense of closure and there certainly were not many answers, in fact there were no answers at all.

CHAPTER SIXTEEN

Talking Italian

I did not get the answers or the relationships I had so desperately wished for from my birth parents, but that did not stop me from loving other people in my life.

I had one of the most prominent romantic relationships of my life in the 90s. We were so in love. We were perfect for each other, however when the arguments started the name calling did too, before he knew the truth of who I was. I loved him so much, I felt like I wanted to tell him the truth as this was my soul mate, we were going to be together forever, so I did.

Do not get me wrong I don't mind a decent argument, but when this soulmate knew he was wrong or that he would not win, his immediate default would be to call me a Paki. Or he would say, it is what you lot are like, there would be many racist terms. That would be the end of the argument because he knew the minute anything to do with the colour of my skin was mentioned I fell apart; my heart shattered and my knees buckled.

How was it possible for someone to look in the eyes of someone they love and come out with such horrendous, hurtful, demeaning names? It broke my heart - I had no defence and he knew it.

I used to ask him why he did it, why he was so hurtful, especially knowing how I felt about the colour of my skin.

And he would say, "Because I know that's the only way to hurt you."

Who does that? Who wants to hurt the person that they say they love that much, so they say the worst things possible? Especially when you know somebody is so in love with you with every part of their body. Why would you want to say these kinds of things? The pain was unbearable at times - it was one thing being hurt from rejection, abandonment and all those things from Tony and Pamela, it was also another thing to be hurt by bullies and racists in society, but this was a completely different pain, a deep, sharper damaging pain. It was a soul shattering pain to hear these words come out of the mouth of someone you gave your heart to, someone who told you that they loved you too. To hear these words out of their mouth was like being struck by a thunderbolt.

The day I left him was the day I vowed never to tell another person my truth in my life unless I was going to marry them. Why would I? If trusting someone with the true knowledge of my heritage, was akin to something I hold inside of me like the Holy Grail, for them to then use it against me was like handing someone a loaded gun and asking them not to shoot me. I could not take that risk again. I could not give someone that much ammunition to use against me and break my heart and destroy my soul again.

Throughout my working life, over the years, I have encountered many, many aspects of racism and it hasn't always been solely directed towards me. I did a job for someone once, who had recently come out of hospital. They told me that one of the most surprising things they found during their stay in his private hospital, was that a white person came to empty his bed pan! (This person had a reasonable amount of money and he thought by paying for private health care he was less likely to be treated by foreign people.

"What's wrong with that?" I said.

"Well, you'd expect a blackie to do that kind of job wouldn't you?" he replied.

To which I replied, "No, of course not, why would you?"

He said "because that's all they're good for - doing the shitty, dirty kind of jobs, clean toilets and things."

We were situated in his workplace. The conversation was then interrupted by his colleague who was late for work. As she walked past us apologising for being late, he responded by saying;

"Oh, it's because you've been with your black boyfriend, isn't it?"

I could not believe what he said, so blatantly and, with no thought or consideration to the language he was using and I saw in his face he meant every word.

I had a few friends in the mid to late 90's, most of them were colleagues, who expressed themselves freely with their opinions about the world and life. Sometimes we went out for drinks; racist jokes would be made and occasionally people would turn to me and say "no offence". It was as though saying that gave them a free pass to spout derogatory, racist opinions or language of their choice. Sometimes after they had finished trying to make themselves look good, through their horrendous tales or jokes, I asked them.

"Why did you say no offence to me?"

They would reply "well you know."

Determined not to make it easy for them, I would reply "what do you mean?"

"You know," they would repeat, however this time they would be point at my face.

Again, I would just try and let them humiliate themselves by asking, "What?" and hold my nose as though there was something on my face.

Then they'd circle their finger over my body. I knew they were referring to the colour of my skin and because they laughed, the other people around the table would join in too. I found it impossible to defend myself, purely because I was outnumbered, and in fear of retaliation or of being bullied.

Once again, I'd find myself saying, "But I'm not a Paki."

"Yes, you are," they would say.

"No, I am not."

"Well, what are you then?" they would ask.

"My father is Italian," I would say knowing that most people did not really have a strong understanding what Italian people looked like, except that the majority had dark hair and dark eyes.

Immediately their demeanour would change and sometimes they apologised for assuming I was of the race that they were making jokes and fun about. And with that I'd be back to being part of the group of people I was with. This happened repeatedly and each time I had to declare, I am not a Paki and to be accepted in the world, usually as soon as I said that everything felt better. People would talk to me they would include me in things. However sometimes if there was an occasion where I was not able to make that declaration, I'd find a lot of people would not even start a conversation with me, if we had mutual friends. Sometimes, strangers would stare, and on occasion people even turned their back on me completely. There have been people that I have started a conversation with and they have just looked at me and turned the other way not even engaging at all. How was I supposed to make people treat me like everyone else? Like every other white person? So, I started making racist jokes of my own, I started laughing at things or commenting on things that people were making fun of, in the hope that they would think well she cannot be a Paki because she said this or said that, or laughed at the jokes.

I dressed in the latest fashions and designer gear and wore short skirts or low tops and had highlights in my hair, I did everything that was as far away from the stereotypical idea of what being Asian looked like to people, so visually they could not connect how I looked to their idea of how Asian people looked in a Sari or a Burka.

Every single morning when I got up, before I left the house, I would have to spend time in front of the mirror deciding how to look that day, what to wear, how to wear my hair, and if anything, or any style looked even slightly Asian it would go in the bin immediately. I stayed with the same hairdresser over the years, despite him moving all over the country. He knew he had free reign over my hair, the only criteria would be "please do what you like, just don't make me look Asian."
Foods that I ate, could not have any spices in, or have any strong smell or taste just in case people would smell garlic or spice or anything on my clothes or breath, further giving course to the belief that they looked at me as non-white.

This whole obsession of me trying to act, talk and look as far removed from my race as possible was sometimes incredibly, debilitating.
In the 90s, despite how I looked and being the owner a model agency I still had people asking me for any girl that does not look foreign.

Blond-haired, blue eyed, white girls, and boys were by far the preferred choice of model by most photographers and companies.

During the past few decades, I remained fearful of going unannounced to meet people, or attend events and parties. If I thought that most people there would be people that already knew me, it was not so bad. But whenever I was introduced to a new person, be it work, friends or even just going to busy clubs or pubs, their first question would nine out of ten times would be, "where are you from?" not 'what you do for a living? Have you travelled far? Have you been here before?'

They could have been the nicest person in the world, but the minute that question came out of their mouths my shutters came down, and chances are I would never speak to that person again. In my mind they were asking that question to then decide if it was within their moral compass to be seen talking to a foreigner, or associating with a Paki. So as usual I would default to 'my father was Italian' however as the years have passed by people's knowledge of what Italians look like became a little savvier, so then I had to change to 'my father is Sicilian' even though it is still part of Italy, it would, instantly throw people off. People even liked it because they would think about the mafia after watching films like the Godfather, and I liked that. I even tried to make it more genuine by taking Italian language lessons and just in case anyone did not believe me, I began speaking in Italian to try and drill home the fact that I was Italian.

Sometimes despite my best efforts, some people I thought were my friends still did not want to be seen out with me, because, if someone wasn't brave enough to ask me directly where I was from, the people I were with would be asked, which then made them feel uncomfortable. The so-called friends were trying to make an informed choice as to whether to carry on drinking with us or not, so, I had to up my game. Whenever I invited someone out for drinks, I always booked a limousine to take us. During the 90s a limousine was considered 'a status symbol' that someone with notoriety would have and it did get attention, however this time it attracted positive attention. People loved to travel in a stretch limousine, most people had never been in one before, so even though we were only going to a local club in Cannock called Silk's, I would pick up my friends in a huge white stretch limousine to take us 4 miles to a club. Along the way we would sip champagne feeling great. It was reminiscent of buying sweets from the tuck shop for people in school to make them want to be my friend, but I found people who would prioritise the love of going in a limousine over them being asked what nationality their friends were.

A large supermarket chain was opening in the West Midlands mid 90's, and I was asked to go along and cut the ribbon, which of course I was happy to do. It meant I had to be at the front of the store by 8:30 AM. As I walked towards the train station on the morning of the event in my high heels and short skirt at 7:30 AM, a young boy walked up to me, he must have been about 14 years old I had never seen him before.

As he approached me, he said, "You are a Paki aren't you?"

I turned my head to look at him, and he whacked me on the top of my head with a short plank of wood then ran away. As I got up from the floor in complete shock, I saw the house that he ran into so I went to the nearest police station and reported it. The police officer did not even take me into a room to take a statement. The person on the desk was a white guy in his 30s, he just said, "There is nothing we can do, its common assault you've got no bruises and you haven't had to go to hospital."

"But it has just happened, he hit me on the top of my head with a plank of wood and I can tell you where he lives," I said.

To which the police officer replied it, "does not matter unless you've had substantial injuries there is nothing we can do, it is common assault," as he shrugged his shoulders.

"He was a child, that child could go and stab someone next week or next year! Surely there is something that can be done," I asked.

"No, sorry" the policeman said "is there anything else we can help you with?"

And that was it, nothing was done. I pondered what kind of world were we in that someone can get away with doing that? I had no bruising yet, or deep cuts, and I did not have to go to hospital. It had just happened and although it was the top of my head, it did not knock me out or cause me severe injury, the point was, the only words the child said was "you are a Paki, aren't you?" and then whacked me, and ran off.

Would things be different today? I do not know. But what I did know is that I was right to pretend I am not who I really was. I was right to continually say 'I am not a Paki'

It was the only way that I could live through each day, I just knew I would be saying this for the rest of my life.

CHAPTER SEVENTEEN

Axe to grind

For over a decade now, the way we communicate has changed. We have mobile phones; social media and the Internet. The world has changed dramatically, and I love the fact we have all these tools of communication. I remember being amazed by fax machines, watching a piece of paper going through a machine, and I thought that same piece of paper, like magic, was coming out of someone else's machine on the other side of the world. I know that's not the case now but I love the fact that if you have friends and families that you don't get chance to see, then you can just write them a letter and email it to them, rather than handwriting messages on bits of paper and posting them off, and having to wait weeks sometimes for replies.

I love that you can stay in touch with people and share photographs and see snapshots into people's lives by using social media. I have quite a few friends who have moved abroad, so to be able to watch how wonderful their life is, I think is the best thing ever.

On the flip side, there are more ways to abuse people and bully people without even the perpetrators being present. It's called trolling.

Trolling, in some ways, is much worse than some of the abuse I had over the years. Mainly because trolls are people you don't know or have never met most of the time. At least when I was at school, people were bullying me to my face, or even as the years have progressed, they would be friends or partners or people in the business. I could see them, and I would mostly know why they were doing it, whether they were showing off in front of their friends, found it funny, or because of things they had seen on the news. However, being sent messages anonymously from someone, whose face you cannot see, or understand why, or even what they wanted to achieve by trolling. I have had DMs, emails, and text messages from people saying horrendous, awful, nasty, racist things. Usually, they are things that are not true and most of the time, I will ignore it. And by ignoring it, I mean I do not reply or respond, but that doesn't mean these things do not transport me back to the 70s and the 80s, and how I was made to feel. Once again, you find people saying to you, 'just ignore them and block them.

Yes, you can block them, and it will stop them from sending you messages from that platform again, but they can create another profile. Ignoring them, it's hard; you can't do that; you can't just ignore something that has had an immediate effect on you. Ignoring something isn't 'a thing'. You cannot unread something, you can't unsee something, you can't even respond to these trolls because they will send a message and then block you. It's almost like knocking on a front door running away, so now there's just another method for people who think it's OK to bully or abuse people because of how they look.

I showed someone a message just last week that had been sent me a couple of years ago. I had no idea who the sender was, why they sent it, or what they wanted to achieve, but what they sent had been vile racist and hurtful. It was sent via social media; the profile it came from either doesn't exist anymore, or I was blocked, I'm not sure. I try not to put too many personal things on social media, not just about race but also about my opinions about whatever is happening in the world. As much as people are entitled to their opinion, sometimes they don't like it, or the people, if they have a difference of opinion to them.

I remember seeing someone troll a friend of mine, and I went on the platform to say, 'no, I know this person, and they are kind and considerate, and then immediately I got abused for posting that. They picked up on the fact that I did not look English. I couldn't cope with it, so how do celebrities and people who have many followers cope with people commenting and trolling on their profiles constantly? I have no idea. I really feel for them; it's hard not to take things personally, so since then, I haven't placed my support or opinion on social media about anything or anyone within reason.

Over the years, I found myself visiting many places worldwide, but even locally, I can get a sense of the place, when visiting some towns or cities. Sometimes, I notice that as I walk through a town, village or even venues such as pubs. I do not see any other people of colour and straight away, it makes me wonder why? I also notice the looks I get, or people exaggerating the walk around me to pass in the street. It was like extreme social distancing of its day. Even as I enter a shop and people hold the door open; if I am walking behind someone, they just let it close on me sometimes. I've tested it a few times. I've let the person I'm with, walk in front of me, and then I've walked into the same shop separately, we receive different reactions. Sometimes, people can just be rude, but it does make you question the difference.

Alternatively, I notice that the opposite happens when visiting countries like Spain or Portugal or holiday destinations such as Sri Lanka or the Caribbean. For example, if my white partner and I go into a local shop abroad, he gets treated differently. Usually, because the locals think I am one of their 'own', they assume that because of my skin colour. Until I speak, of course, and then they know differently. So, that is possibly one of the only times that my colour gets a positive response.

My circle is small these days, and I have a couple of girlfriends of colour, they are mainly Jamaican and Caribbean, who used to go to a local bar. It was nothing special, but we always used to have a good time there it was predominantly people of colour who used to drink in there.

One of these friends I absolutely adored from the minute I met her, I don't know what it was, but I just love being around her. We always have a laugh, and I just like her energy. When I found out she was half Indian, I was gobsmacked. I thought she was part Jamaican.

One night we went to said bar and sat outside as it was a nice evening. There must have been around 40 people standing on the terrace. This friend knows absolutely everyone, everywhere we go or anyone we see, she knows them, and I love that. However, this evening, someone who stood about 15 feet away from us in another group of people shouted hello to my friend, and she replied back. I didn't think anything of it because it was a usual situation when we were all together, but the person continued their conversation across the terrace and over the heads of people. They asked about someone, and this man thought he had the wrong person, so to clarify, he asked my friend If her mother was Jamaican. So, my friend shouted across e terrace in front of all these people. "No, my mum's Indian."

The man replied, "Oh, I must have the wrong person" or something similar.

I didn't hear the rest of the conversation. I was just stared at my friend and looked around, saying to myself, 'how did she just do that?' 'How did she just shout in front of everyone, without blinking, "no, my mom is Indian." And not one person in the whole place batted an eyelid. There was no change in atmosphere or anything.

My friend became my hero that night. Never in my life to date have

I ever been able to do anything remotely like that. Never in my life have I ever thought about saying that to a person standing next to me, let alone across a bar. All night in my head, I was repeating over and over again, how did she do that? How the fuck did she do that? I never told her I was in awe of her that night. But even now, I have so much love for her for being able to say her truth so openly. I think I will love her for the rest of my life because of that. If only I was that resilient and robust.

I felt hate towards Asian people mainly because I was one of them. Because I was bullied and abused, and my life has been horrendous. It's almost like if you get bitten by a dog, you try and avoid dogs. If you have a seafood allergy, you avoid seafood. My avoidance and lack of acknowledgement to the Asian race was born out of the life I was made to lead.

I didn't like feeling that way. I'm certainly not proud of it, but it was so ingrained that denying being who I was meant I led a much safer, more acceptable, happier life. I know it is wrong. I know I am supposed to be proud of where I'm from and my roots and heritage. But how could I be? The source of my heritage had given me a life of pain, destruction and heartache and destroyed my soul. I always asked myself get through the rest of my life feeling like this?

Fifteen years ago, I was travelling back home one night in my brand-new car. As I was drove up one of the main roads leading back into the city, around 7:30pm. I looked across the road to my right, and I saw a group of people stood outside a house on the footpath. There must have been about 30 people, and there was one white man covered head to toe in blood, and he was swinging an axe at two Asian boys who were jumping back so as not to get hit by the weapon. There were lots of shouting and screaming. I could not believe what I was seeing; it was like a scene from the Texas Chainsaw Massacre. I immediately swung my car around the island and back towards this scene. The crowd were all jeering the white guy on whilst standing behind him. I have always acted fearless and without thought in many unjust situations to a point, and this was one of them.

I mounted the curb in my car, banging my horn as loudly as I could whilst trying to dial the police on speaker phone. As I ascended the kerb, the crowd dispersed a little and right in front of me was the white guy, his head stained with blood and his tee-shirt blood-soaked, holding the axe above his head, ready to take another swing; he turned and stared at me. For a split second, I thought, he was going to smash my new car, but I continued holding down the horn as I talked to the police. Within minutes the police came with a dog van, and everything; until then, I kept revving my engine and banging my horn to distract the man from swinging down the axe again, hoping he would think I would run him over for what he was doing. I did not know what the situation was about; all I saw was this one man and now a gang of people attacking two boys. As soon as the police came, the crowd dispersed. I told the police what I saw and gave them my details as they took the man away and the two boys.

"We might need you to come to the police station to make a statement," they told me.

"That's fine," I said. So, I gave them my details, and I left.

As I was driving home, the adrenaline started to subside, and then the emotion kicked in at the thought of what could have happened. At best, my car would have been smashed up; at worst, I could have been killed, and so could those two young Asian boys. What just happened I thought to myself, none of it made sense, I had so much hatred towards the Asian race, and yet without thinking, I just literally risked my life to save two young Asian boys from being killed. I was so confused I was arguing with myself in my head, trying to make sense of it. But it wouldn't matter what the colour of their skin had been; the act of a man swinging an axe with the jeering crowd behind him regardless of what it was about was wrong. So that fearless fighter inside me overruled the person trying to be racist.

For weeks, I could not make sense of this. Had I had some kind of shift inside me? I do not know.

I had to go to court as a witness to what had happened, it was my first court experience, and the man was charged with attempted murder. The judge praised me for my actions and stated that the two boys may have lost their lives without my intervention that day. It wasn't until I left court that I found out these people were neighbours, and the whole thing was over a parking space outside their house. I never did find out the sentence the man received.

These days, despite having lived over half a century on this earth, I still face racism; you would think it would decrease as you become older. But it hurts more because most people who make racist comments are adults. So, I am assuming they are very much aware and in control of what they say, for the most part, it hurts more. At least with children, they have no awareness of the consequences of their words at a young age, but as an adult, I'm pretty sure that these kinds of people who abuse me know precisely what they are saying and why they're saying it. They cannot hide behind naivety, or lack of knowledge, of what they're saying.

A couple of years ago, I went to a local market with my sister. We were waiting for someone to pull out of a parking space, to which point someone else drove in front of us and into the space we were waiting for. As we found another space and parked up, we saw the people getting out of the previous car.

My sister said, "We were waiting to drive into that space."

"No, you weren't," the lady replied.

She was a lady in her 50s who had a couple of people with her in their early 20s and about two young children who I am assumed were daughters and grandchildren.

I said to her, "yes, she was, you could see she was indicating."

The woman turned to me and immediately responded, "no one was talking to you, you fat black wog."

Once again, not for the first time in my life, I felt like my whole breath, and my words had been ripped out of my body. Nothing came out of my mouth. I think I was even stood there with my mouth wide open, completely frozen in shock. The lady and her family walked away, and the only thing that I could get out of my mouth was, "what a wonderful role model you must be for your kids."

My sister and I went to the cafe, and I sat there in absolute shock. I hadn't heard that word for years; my sister couldn't believe it either. How could someone in today's world get away with saying those words in a public place? I've got to report her. I said I had to; she must be the matriarch of that family, and if the kids didn't blink an eye at her saying that to a stranger, then what else must be going on in their house, she cannot be allowed to get away with that. It is a crime these days to make racist comments.

I knew a policeman usually walked around the market, so I set off to find him. I saw the policeman up ahead, and as I approached him, he turned around, he was black, at that moment I didn't know whether to tell him or not. I didn't want him to feel some way, as he will have probably been through things similar himself. But at the same time, I was hoping he would also understand why I was so upset, not just because he was of colour too, but he was a policeman, and it was his job to act on this kind of complaint surely.

I told him what had happened, and he said, "Do you know where she is now?"

"No," I replied, "but she can't be far."

"OK," he said ", do you know the registration of the car."

"No, but I will go into the car park now and get it," I said.

I raced off to the car, to get the registration number; there's no getting away from it. I approached the car park spot she stole, it was empty. She must have made the quickest visit to the market ever. It was about half an hour since it happened. Maybe she saw me talking to the policeman and made a quick exit.

I returned to the policeman and told him the car had gone. I knew there was nothing else we could do. The lady had greying hair, glasses, and was about 5 foot 4. She was in her 50s and, of course, white. This description described 70% of the people that visit the market. I knew the chances of seeing her or finding her again were remote. She must have carried on her life to abuse the next person.

It wasn't until reflecting later on, that I asked myself, if people would find what happened insignificant in their eye? She just called me a horrible name, but in my eyes, the term that she used, and the viciousness behind it, was what has led me to live this life in pain and heartbreak and suffering for the whole of my life.

Is this how whatever remains of my life on this earth will continue to be?

CHAPTER EIGHTEEN

Desperately seeking Susan

I did not like feeling the anger I did. I felt it was getting much worse as time passed by, I needed to get help, I had to at least try and overcome the constant feeling of persecution. I had tried speaking to people about my situation. I have been referred for counselling by my GP many times. The first therapist I saw was an Asian man in his 50s. I found it impossible to sincerely open up my heart and admit that I had a problem with his race, and by his race, I meant my race too. All I could really tell him was that I was down and depressed.

His response was; "How many times a week do you have sex? How often? Who do you have sex with? How many times and what was it like?"

I never saw him again. I tried again a few years later, and again it was an Asian therapist! I could not tell him the real reasons I had issues.

Then a friend told me about a two-day course that was happening in London, and that was all about positive thinking.

She said to me, "I have to tell you everything that happens in my life because you are the most negative person I know, so you will always tell me the worst-case scenario."

Marvellous, I thought. So, when my friend told me about this course, despite it being quite expensive, I agreed to go. There must have been about 400 people attending the seminar. The lecturer reminded me of a 'Tony Robbin's' man. The topic was all about predictive thinking and predicting what we think people are thinking, which is not always the case. He challenged anyone in the audience to stand up and tell him what their concerns were, and he would change the way they thought about them, ultimately changing their life and perception of situations they were in. One by one, people raised their hands and stood up. They opened up about their problems in front of everyone, highlighting topics such as divorce or being unfulfilled in a job. I soaked up everything he said and the little tasks he set us to do were fabulous. Everything seemed very positive, and I found myself engrossed in his every word; everything made perfect sense.

The two friends I had travelled to London with for this course were blonde, blue-eyed white girls. I wanted to be the person that put their hand up during this lecture and speak out about my problem. However, I couldn't because the two girls with me knew nothing, and they thought I was Italian. Furthermore, the whole audience was of mixed race, and all different walks of life, which was another reason I could not speak up in fear of the consequences of doing so from other audience members.

On the second day, the speaker claimed that being on the course would change all our lives, "everything will be different once you leave here," he said.

That was a bold statement, I thought, especially as the only way my life would be different was if I had white skin according to my experiences in life to that date. He certainly did not have a magic wand to make that happen.

The end of the course came, by then it all made sense. He explained exactly what I should do if I met someone, and the first thing they asked me was where I was from. Usually, I assume they ask this because they don't want to be seen with a Paki, then I continue to assume that they make a judgement on the fact that if I am one, I would blow up the house, or I am dirty, or I own some shops, or I'm not worthy of being in their company - a whole load of things. Whereas in reality, they might actually be thinking, I wonder where she's from because she has lovely skin, or I wonder where she is from because she's attractive, or mostly they would ask that question as an ice breaker to start a conversation. So, everything the speaker said all kind of made sense, and it was true that maybe when somebody asked that question, I predicted that what they were thinking about me was negative.

I'd never thought about this before. People did ask me because they do not know what else to say. People are simply curious, so alternatively they could start a conversation with 'oh, I have been to that country,' or something like that. This was wonderful. This new way was enlightening for me. After having my way of thinking for so long, how could I put this into practice? Could I change my whole way of thinking?

At the end of the course, the lecturer said again, "your lives will be different once you leave here."

People started to put their hands up and give him examples of how they already felt differently. I did not have that feeling. 'Oh my God! I'd spent over 500 pounds on this course, and I had not changed; it hadn't worked.' So once the course had finished, I approached the lecturer and said to him amongst many other people trying to talk to him too.

"I've enjoyed your course, but I don't feel any different," I said.

To which he replied, "Just go back to your life and see."

"But I don't feel it," I said.

And he repeated, "Just go back to your life, and you'll see."

It was time for us to make our way back home. Just before we left for the train station, I called in to the local shop to grab a few things for the journey. The shop was bustling, as everyone from the course had left simultaneously. I looked into the shop, and it seemed to be full of Asians, but we didn't have time to go and find a new shop, so I went in. I walked to the back of the shop to get some water out of the fridge. Unfortunately, I had to pass by a group of about 6 Asian boys who were blocking the aisle.

"Excuse me," I said, as I waited for them to make space for me to walk past.

"Sorry," they said, this was an automatic response to people saying excuse me, and they moved so as I could access the fridge.

I paid for my water and left. Then it hit me, as soon as I left that shop. I said to my two friends, "Oh my God, I cannot believe what just happened."

"What?" they replied.

"I just went in that shop, and I said excuse me to a group of Asians so I could pass by" I explained.

My friends looked at me confused, as to what was the problem.
"What's wrong with that?" they said.

"I have never done that before," I replied.

Still confused they said.

"I don't get it?"

I replied, "Well, usually I just push them out the way, I'm never as polite to them."

I felt like some miracle had occurred, I felt like the speaker in the lecture had cursed us all. We sat on the train back home in wonder. Maybe my life would be different after all. Perhaps I am my own worst enemy for predicting what people really thought of me.

The miracle didn't last too long, as I still found myself in situations where it was noticeably clear what people thought, people still using the name Paki. People were still talking about 'terrorists' in the street, and on the TV. Just when I thought I'd had some fabulous intervention in my life and a miracle had occurred. I had experienced a kind of respite in my thought processes; but the negativity and the confirming racist actions of the people outnumbered the positives.

Because I had this very brief spell of feeling better about things, it worsened my depression and anxiety. I had those experiences of positivity and a positive mind, which made the negativity much deeper. I was angry all of the time, against the world, angry against things that were happening in the news, with myself, and I hated myself. I didn't like feeling the way that I did but because of the colour of my skin, it was never going to end. I tried counselling again a few times with no success.

Now we have different media platforms where people unashamedly post their views football games were being televised, this meant there's millions of people who get exposed to monkey chants towards players on the pitch. People have phones with them all of the time, so the minute something is happening it's being filmed and being posted on a platform, which is shared by millions of people. I was at the point where I was so angry, I thought I would end up hurting someone or myself. I had to try counselling again, I was already on antidepressants and anxiety tablets.

I went back to my doctor.

"I need to see someone," I said to my doctor. "I feel like I'm in a closed darkroom searching for a light switch, and I just cannot find it."

I had to explain to her that I needed to see a white therapist.

"Sorry I cannot guarantee that," she said.

I explained that I had tried therapy many other times, but the therapists had all been Asian and so I had been unable to open up to them about my situation. In turn I hadn't been able to get the help I needed.

"They have to be a white person," I said, "I cannot sit in front of an Asian therapist and tell them that people the same colour as they are, have caused me so much pain, and then open up to them about those situations."

"I will try," she said, "But there's a long waiting list to get therapy."
It was almost a year before I had an appointment to go and see someone. During this time my feelings were getting worse and worse. I was more worried as I'd asked for help and had to wait so long to receive it. Anything could have happened in that time.

The appointment day had arrived, I was seen by a white lady who looked to be in her 40s. I explained my reasons for needing help, she replied with, "Well, I'm not your therapist, I'm just a counsellor who decides if you need therapy or not."

I felt like I was back to square one again, so I reiterated that I needed a white therapist.

"We don't have one," she said.

"Well, this is ridiculous, I am trying to reach out for help; I am asking for help and you cannot give it to me," I said.

She replied with, "but they are all therapists, they will still be able to help you."

She clearly had no understanding of what I was saying.

"You have to see one of the people after me, and then I pass you on to the relevant therapist," she said.

"Ok," I said, "are they white?"

"No," she replied.

For fucks sake I was getting nowhere.

"There's nothing else I can do," she said, "she is lovely, she will understand."

"But you do not understand," I said, "how can I sit in front of her, and say I have a problem with your race, I have a problem because I am like you?"

"I can be there with you," she said.

"That does not help; why can't you just tell her for me?" I asked
"That's the only way for you to get real help," she said.

I waited outside her office for a space to become free with the therapist, who could then refer me to the appropriate therapist. As I went into the office, I saw she was an Asian lady in her 50s. So I sat down with the previous white counsellor.

"How can we help?" said the therapist.

"Well, I need to see someone," I said.

"What's is the problem?" she said.

I just stared at the counsellor sitting next to me, urging her to speak on my behalf, as she said she would. But, instead, she was just stared back at me. I actually wanted to punch her in her face because she did not say anything. I felt like she got me in there with lies and threw me under the bus.

"You said you would speak for me," I said to her.

"It has to come from," you she said.

I have never felt like smacking someone in the face more in my life, so I started to explain to the therapist. The therapist made some notes but did not make eye contact with me. I cannot imagine what she must have been thinking.

"I have to see a white person," I said. "I do not want to waste anyone's time."

"We do not have a white therapist," she said.

Then the therapist and the counsellor started talking between themselves, trying to think of therapist names who may be white and able to help. This was ridiculous, I thought, surely there must be white counsellors or therapists otherwise, I was subjecting myself to live this way for whatever time I will left on this earth.

"Leave it with us, and we will see what we can do, but you may have to wait longer until we can find a white person who becomes free," they said.

"That is fine," I replied.

Another year went by, and eventually, an appointment landed on my doormat. Christopher Bird, well that sounded English, but you could not be sure these days, as even my father used an English name. I telephoned the clinic and enquired, they confirmed he was indeed a white Englishman and so my therapy started.

"Good luck" were the first words I said to him.

He must have been in his late 20s but, he was white so that was enough for me to give him a chance. I went to see him twice a week for three months, he asked me why I felt I had to lie when people asked where I was from. I explained everything to him.

"But you do not have to tell them anything," he said.

"Yes, I do, because people ask and ask over and over until I tell them," I said.
"Just tell them you are English, which you are," he said.

"But that is not enough," I tried to explain.

He went on to explain to me how sometimes we only allow our heads things that confirm what we already think, and we bounce away things that do not fit into that circle. I liked him; he was very clever. He definitely did not fix me, but it made me think differently.

Since then, I do not tell people anything when they ask. It is not as often I get asked these days but when I do, I do not tell them anything.

I moved to New York City, USA, for a while. This was a huge turning point for me, people in New York saw me as white! This was music to my ears, whenever people were cracking jokes or saying something that was a little bit racist, I would say to them, "you do realise that I am not white?"

"Yes, you are," they would say.

Well, that was a shift in behaviour - there I was trying to convince somebody that I was a person of colour, and they were trying to convince me that they actually saw me as white. This still continues to amuse me to this day. We all know that some Americans don't like the Mexicans, and that is their bugbear over there. But to them I was white! I could walk down the street and around the streets of New York and not once did I ever hear a racist name or remark towards me, not once, no one saw the colour of my skin as brown at all. This blew my mind, and for the first time in the whole of my life I felt free, I felt like I was walking on clouds. My mind was clear, my heart was beating and my soul felt warm. The only time I have ever felt similar feelings was when I was on holiday in the Maldives, I was just on an island in the middle of the ocean with no more than 200 other people from all countries. I felt like I had been born again. It was the happiest I had ever felt in my life, it was almost like I had an inner calm. New York life is hard, but that got offset with the inner peace I carried in my heart and soul, day after day. My mom became quite poorly and I had to return to the UK.

On the flight home a lady was sitting next to me on the plane.

"Oh, you have lovely skin," she said.

"Thank you," I replied - the weather had been scorching hot in the states so I had obtained a nice golden tan. I didn't know what was to come.

"Where are you from?" she said, and there it was.

"England," I replied.

"No, where are you really from?" she asked again. In my mind all I could think of was, no please no please, please, no. I replied "the Midlands."

"No, I mean where are you really from? She said thinking saying it twice made her clearer.

It had been a while since I had to put up with this kind of conversation. "Wolverhampton," I said.

"No, where are your parents from?"

"Wolverhampton," I said nodding, hoping she would realise she was not going to get the answer she was looking for.

"No, I mean where in the world?"

She was not going to give up, so I had to try and embarrass her, thinking of my therapist saying you do not have to tell anyone.

"My mother is blonde and blue-eyed" I said.

"Ah, so it's your father, where is your father from?"

"I am English," I replied.

"Yes, but your father must have dark skin, where's his family from?" She was trying everything she possibly could rather than just come out with 'are you a Paki?'

She went on and on and on, finding every other way to ask the same question, in the end, I pretended I needed the toilet, and I stayed in there for about 10 minutes, until I heard the drinks cart coming around. Knowing that would be a distraction for her for a brief time, I asked the cabin crew if there were any other spaces I could move to in the plane.

"No sorry we are full" she replied and just like that I felt like I had been taken back in time.

I sat back down next to the lady and quickly put on my headphones and watched the first film that came up on the TVs in front of us until we landed.

We are in the age of Black Lives Matter, and with social media people are exposed to so many more injustices, not just in our home country but around the world too. The whole George Floyd situation rippled across the world, and everybody wanted to stand for justice, well not everyone. I had a fair few followers on my social media, thousands of people who see what I post on a day-to-day basis, and I see what they post on a day-to-day basis too.

So, when the whole George Floyd thing happened, so many people were posting their support for justice, their support to eradicate racism, their support for sports people to take the knee, and it was great had we finally had a move towards getting rid of racism? Not just in this country but around the world too? It was wonderful to see. There were the occasional people that would post something negative, but mostly there were good posts. People enjoy a bandwagon, but as the days turned into weeks and the weeks into months and people were still talking about BLM you could see people's masks were starting to fall on socials.

'Are they still going on about this?'

"Fed up with hearing about this now."

'Are we going to have to take the knee for the rest of our lives before games now?'

'For fucks sake, he was just a black man, doing wrong."

One by one we started to see the masks falling to the floor, and people's real opinions started showing.

Does this mean people are happy to end racism, but only just for a few months a year because some of the population lose interest of its longer than that?

People started pulling down statues around the country. You saw a difference in the media's headlines, with two groups of people doing the same thing. One group was mainly black, the other was prominently white, and the headlines would read entirely differently. The group of black people were called terrorists, packs rioting. The white group were called protestors standing up for their rights and beliefs. We saw news reports of people dying on their journeys crossing the channel as they came to a better life in the UK. Responses to that on social media lit up with people commenting, things like, "coming over here taking our jobs and draining our system", people even posted memes laughing at people that had died in their journey to the UK. Let us hope that these racists do not find themselves in a situation where they literally have to escape their country in fear for their lives.

I have been involved with a massive event mainly aimed at black people for many years. This event is attended by many celebrities and also gets broadcast onto the TV. One year I was tasked with sorting out the after-party for all the winners of the awards and celebrities. There were so many clubs in London who are happy to let us use their venue for free as the publicity they would get and the calibre of the people attending was huge, they promised me everything as they showed me around their clubs. Until I mentioned the name of the event which made them realise there would be a lot of black people attending the party. Immediately the venue was no longer available. Two weeks it took me to find a venue that were happy for us to hold the after-show there. A few days before the event was due to happen the manager of the venue asked for meeting where he requested, "it will be a mix though won't it? Please don't let it be too dark?" he said.

"What?" I replied, "What does that mean?"

"Well, you know, we do not want any trouble, so please just keep a good mix but edging on more white people," he said.

"Should I get a Dulux colour chart? And match them against people's skin colour as they come in?" I said trying to be sarcastic.

"No, but you know, we have got to think about security and the look of the club," He replied.

It was the day before the event, and it was too late for me to find another club. Needless to say, I did not make any changes to the guest list at all, but what was most surprising was the attitude of this venue. Even more surprising is that resident DJ is an incredibly famous person of colour. I was so tempted to expose their messages and emails but once again I did not feel I was strong enough to cope with the abuse I expected to get back.

A lot of us see racism, or acts of racism most days. Whether that's opinions on socials or jokes that people find funny. Even things that people sell in shops, everyday businesses must make inclusive decisions. We all saw the advertisements from big players in retail who have included more people of colour than ever before. Whilst this is a good thing, but I wonder are they doing it for the right reasons or just ticking boxes now?

Before writing this book, I spoke to several people about their experiences with racism. I. even questioned some businesses about their recruitment policies. They told me that if they have two people apply for a job with the same qualifications, they are having to make decisions based on the colour of their skin. Sometimes regardless of experience just so they can tick the box that they are not a racist company.

I am lucky to have a job where I have a platform that I offer to people to talk about experiences in their lives, not just racism, but if they are different to other people, either through the colour of their skin, physical differences, or mental health. With a view to ideally helping others who may be going through something similar.

I also spoke to a couple ladies who have very prominent jobs in society, these two ladies had brown skin and they wore a hijab. I asked one lady who was in her early 20s what her experience of racism was. She told me she had never experienced any racism in her life. I nearly fell off my chair "pardon," I said "what kind of school did you go to?" She told me she went to a school where only two people were white.

The second lady told me the only racism she had experienced was when she moved to this country from Germany, and it was not long after the 7/7 attacks in London. She said someone came behind her in the street, and pulled off her hijab, pulling her to the ground. Then she told me how within seconds there were a group of 10 white people who created a wall between her and her attacker.

Before writing this book, I had to 'come out' to a few people who I hold dear and class as close friends, because they too did not know my true origin. Most of them told me stories that they have experienced with racism in the recent years, and mostly with members of their own family.

We are products of our environments, for the most part. If you grow up in a household who are all fans of football, then chances are you will be a football fan too. So, in my opinion if you grow up in a racist household, then you may share that same opinions or values until hopefully you reach an age where you can have your own opinions and views.

I have had people tell me that their families have had to move house to a completely different town or city because they had Indians move into the house next door to them.

Things are a little bit different these days, no one raises their eyebrows so much now when we see mixed-race couples shopping. We even see mixed crowds celebrating Diwali, and other religious festivals.

Someone sent me a story not so long ago about a lady who thought and believed she was not racist. This lady who was a very busy person, someone of notoriety, was waiting to pull into a parking bay, she could see a car trying to pull out of a spot, the windows were blacked out and the music was playing, she assumed the driver must be a black man. They were spending so long trying to get out of this spot that the lady waiting was getting impatient, for fucks sake, she would say in her head she was getting more and more angry and impatient as the driver of the car took so long to pull out of a spot going forward and reversing, going forward and reverse so many times. The lady was losing her patience. Eventually the driver of the parked car pushed the window down to get a clearer view of what was behind them. It was then she noticed the driver was actually a little old white man. Everything changed instantly. Her demeanour had changed, 'Aww, bless him trying to get out of a parking spot, shall I get out and see if he wants any help?' were the thoughts that went through her head. Then she just sat calmly, patiently waiting for the little old white man to pull out of the spot. She continued to say that's when she caught herself. That's when she realised that she had some form of prejudice inside of her that she hadn't recognised before. She then went home and told her father what had just happened, to which he replied.

"Well, there's very few black people that can drive well, what did you expect?" he said to her.

That's when she realised that this internal racism must have come from her family.

I hear so many stories of people catching themselves saying or doing something without thinking. Well, that comes from somewhere, either you are constantly walking around with a mask of your own or you need to look at yourself.

There are very few high streets you see today that do not have Chinese takeaways, Indian, Turkish and Lebanese restaurants to name a few. The UK is a multicultural country, which is great but that does not mean there are no racists. My experience dictates that racists are usually in plain sight, and I do not believe that we will eradicate racism in mine or your lifetime. We are talking about stopping racism as a world now, but the words you use have to match what is in your heart.

Actions must have integrity. It has to be more than just liking a post on social media. It must be more than choosing not to purchase an item because you feel it has racist cogitations. It has to be more than having token friends of colour. There is nothing to be gained by pretending you are not a racist, instead look into yourself and establish where those thoughts come from or why you had a certain opinion or action and own it, and change it.

Am I fixed? Absolutely not. But for me to write this book and tell the world who I really am has been one of the hardest things I have ever done. But the world feels like it is a different place from what it was in the 70s and 80s. It feels safer to tell people the truth of who I am. Since making the decision to write this book I have not hidden who I am. And who knows maybe one day I will actually try a curry.

In the meantime, I just want to live in a world where I will never say "I am not a Paki."

Connect with me

If my story has moved or inspired you and you'd like to know more, you can reach out to me here:

FaceBook: https://www.facebook.com/IamSusanVickers/

Twitter: https://twitter.com/susanvickers1

Instagram: https://www.instagram.com/supersusan/

Linkedin: https://www.linkedin.com/in/ladysusanvickers/

Website: susanvickers.com

Email: susan@susanvickers.com